PLAYS
of the
ITALIAN THEATRE

PLADS

of the

ITALIAN THEATRE

VERGA, MORSELLI, LOPEZ,
PIRANDELLO

Translated by
ISAAC GOLDBERG, PH.D.

One-Act Play Reprint Series

Core Collection Books, inc.
GREAT NECK, NEW YORK

First Published 1921
Reprinted 1976

PQ
4244
E6
P56

International Standard Book Number
0-8486-2009-7

Library of Congress Catalog Number
76-40394

PRINTED IN THE UNITED STATES OF AMERICA

To
CHARLES HALL GRANDGENT
Professor of Romance Languages
in Harvard University

INTRODUCTION

Among the features that make the study of Italian drama so interesting are the diversity of the types, the numerous differences that divide the critics and the more or less diffuse state in which the institution still finds itself. We are prepared for the cry of decadence that has filled half of the nineteenth century and not a little of the twentieth; to be a dramatic critic is almost synonymous, in all tongues, with bewailing the low state into which the drama has fallen. In Italy the matter has gone much farther; there have not been lacking scholars who deny the existence of a genuinely national stage, and since Tullio Fornioni, in 1885, started the ball a-rolling it has been given powerful shoves by such writers as Mario Pilo, Salvatore Barzilai and V. Morello. Only this year Signor Guido Ruberti, in his closely packed two-volume book upon "Il Teatro Contemporaneo in Europa," renews the discussion and in his section upon the realistic Italian drama (I,211) declares bluntly, "The truth is that Italy has never had a truly national theatre." He goes on to state, in the ensuing commentary, that there is, in the very nature of the Italian people, a certain quality that is anti-dramatic in effect; the spiritual and material difficulties experienced by the nation while other countries were conquering a greater or less degree of liberty caused it to turn in upon itself, accustoming it perforce to a "singular mental habit of adaptation and conciliation; a remarkable equilibrium that succeeds in fusing within itself the most diverse tendencies, harmonizing them in a supreme ideal which is neither skepticism nor austere faith, neither absolute indifferentism nor unreflecting passion, yet feeds upon and communicates all these." The Italian conscience, moreover, unlike the Anglo-Saxon and the Slav, finds its great problems settled in advance by its creed, thus removing, or at least greatly modifying, one of the mainsprings of dramatic action. In the powerful scenes of passionate crime the critic sees but added proof of the primitiveness of his people; upon them, he tells us, the currents of modern thought make little impression.

For much of the delay in the achieving of a national theatre the influence of France is blamed, the same France in whom Spanish-American critics fear a similar denationalizing influence and who, according to Brazilian writers, is Gallicizing the immense Portuguese-speaking republic to our south. Again, the presence of so many well defined regions, each with its own psychology, its own pride, its own determination to preserve its spiritual autonomy, acts as a hindrance to the formation of a distinctly recognizable national drama. The Italian dialect stage is an important institution; Rome, Sicily, Milan, Bologna, Venice, Naples — these are, from the dramatic standpoint, fairly nations within a nation, and even the better known Italian dramatists

are proud to write for them. Of the writers represented in this collection, for example, Verga and
Pirandello are intimately related to their native
Sicily, as is Sabatino Lopez to his Tuscan birth-
place.

If, then, it is yet a problem whether Italy's drama
be truly national as an institution, there is far less
doubt as to whether good plays have been written by
Italians; the stage flourishes, even if at times the
native product is strangely absent. And in this
activity the part of the one-act play is singularly
important, as the Italian audience is used to wit-
nessing more than one play a night, and has a fond-
ness for the curtain-raiser. Of late there has arisen
the custom of devoting an entire evening to a pro-
gram of one-act plays, so that the native playwrights
consider the short form a legitimate and worthy
object of their endeavor, approaching it with conscience and interest. They have imparted to the
concentrated drama all the various novelties that
have come out of France and the North; now it is a
bit of unacclimated Ibsenism, as in Giacosa's
"Diritti dell' anima," again, the latest type of
cerebralized thriller as in F. Maria Martini's "Ridi,
Pagliaccio"; Marinetti, indeed, in his futuristic
orgasms, has evolved a type of drama that requires
but a page or two of print.

The plays included in this collection have been
chosen primarily for readableness and accessibility
to the taste and resources of the small theatre audience and producer.

CONTENTS

GIOVANNI VERGA

(1840—   )

The octogenarian figure of Giovanni Verga is intimately associated, in the history of Italian letters, with the movement that is known in the peninsula as "verismo," and out of it as realism and naturalism. Verism, of course, has its distinguishing characteristics, but it is part of the great anti-romantic reaction and in Verga found such vigorous, artistic expression that even today more than one of the "young" writers is not ashamed to acknowledge the influence of the aged dean. Labels have mattered little to him. "Words, words, words," he once said. "Naturalism, psychologism! There's room for everything, and the work of art may be born of any 'ism'. Let it be born — that is the main thing!" The man has always been of a retiring disposition, disliking the appelation "verist" as much as Ibsen ever hated the term Ibsenite; indeed, when a year ago his country honored him on his eightieth birthday, many thought that he had died long before, and they had to be informed all over again that his "I Malavoglia" (1881) was one of the best novels of its century, and that its author was one of the most solid glories of latter-day Italian literature. That he was the author of the intense "Cavalleria Rusticana" (Rustic Chivalry) out of which was made the

I

libretto of Mascagni's melodious opera was matter of more common knowledge. Yet Verga's position as a playwright, if we except this dramatization of one of his own Sicilian tales, is secondary.

He was born in Catania, and began his career as a writer of conventional novels redolent of the French feuilletons. Yet in a deeper sense the work of Verga is a psychological unity, and close study of the early books shows the young Verga to be father to the older. The novel that caps his creations, "I Malavoglia," was intended to be the first of a trilogy devoted to a study of what he named "the vanquished" (*i vinti*) but after the second of the series, "Don Mastro-Gesualdo," he appears to have given up the project, unless, as a French critic has suggested, we are to take his novel "Dal Tuo al Mio" (later made by him into a play) as the closing volume.

There seems, in Verga's work, to be a certain parallel to the labors of that Thomas Hardy whose life, too, runs parallel to the great Italian's. In both the same underlying pessimism, in both the same softening pity. An Italian critic, Carlo Linati, has also suggested Verga's affinity to Synge, for his deep insight into the lives of the humble fishermen. By these tokens we are in the presence of an enduring figure whose influence among the more serious of the newer novelists is strong and salutary.

Verga's atmosphere is naturally in good measure that of his native scene, where life is lived amidst a ferocious intensity of passions and a powerful belief in fate. His so-called impersonality should not mislead his readers, however. "It is not to satisfy a Flaubertian esthetics," writes Luigi Russo in his recent book upon Verga, "that the author of 'Cavalleria Rusticana' tries not to intervene in his tale; it is because his model, the Sicilian peasant, is convinced that he himself does not intervene in the conduct of his own life."

Guido Ruberti, in his new book upon "Il Teatro Contemporaneo in Europa," accords to the stage version of "Cavalleria Rusticana" an importance to Italian dramaturgy comparable to the significance of "I Malavoglia" to the Italian novel. "The entire theatrical production of Giovanni Verga," he writes, "is contained in a little volume of pocket size, about four hundred pages long; yet there will come a day when we'll go back to it to discover inside the sincerest and most artistic representation of life that our theatre produced toward the close of the nineteenth century."

The sketch included in this collection was published in 1902. Verga's other plays include "In Portineria" (At The Porter's Lodge), "La Lupa" (The She-Wolf), "Dal Tuo al Mio" (Thine and Mine).

PERSONS.

LOLLO.   MARIANGELA.

BELLAMÀ.

THE WOLF-HUNT

A Dramatic Sketch

———

SCENE: *A shepherd's hut. A night of wind and rain — the time when wolves are abroad. From the entrance door, at the left, comes the sound of repeated knocking.*

MARIANGELA.

[*All upset, and but half dressed, hurriedly closing the kitchen door.*]

I'm coming! I'm coming! I'm in bed. A moment till I dress.

> [*At last she goes to open the door and finds herself face to face with Lollo, dripping water, his gun in hand and his countenance grim. For a moment he stands rigidly upon the threshold, looking about with restless, suspecting eyes. Outside the tempest rages. The wife, confronted by her husband at this unwonted hour, in such weather, and noting his strange looks, begins to quiver like a leaf, and can scarcely summon the strength to stutter:*]

5

What happened? What's the trouble?

[*He does not answer, not even with an oath. He is a man of few words, particularly when in an ugly mood. He grumbles unintelligibly and continues to peer out of his troubled eyes into every corner. The lamp is upon the table; the bed made as it should be; the door to the kitchen is crossed by a bar, within are cocks and hens, scared by the storm, as might be expected, and making a great hubbub. The poor wife's confusion is increased by all this, and she dares not even look into her husband's face.*]

Good Lord! What a fright you gave me!

LOLLO.

[*First of all he closes the door securely, then hangs his hood upon a hook and wipes the gun-lock with his handkerchief. He mutters.*]

Oh, fine! So I frighten you, do I? Your own husband scares you now?

MARIANGELA.

In this terrible storm! Has there been some accident in the sheepfold? How do you happen to come back at this hour?

LOLLO.

[*Circling about here and there, slowly, like a spectre, dragging along his peasant shoes, poking the muzzle of his gun into every nook. His wife follows him about, in anxiety.*]

I'm going about my affairs. Let me have some
light there, behind the bed. What the devil are you
shivering about? Haven't you enough courage in
you tonight to hold the lamp straight?

MARIANGELA.

[*Uneasily.*]

Can't you tell me what you're looking for?

LOLLO.

Let me have light, I say.

MARIANGELA.

See, there's nothing here.

LOLLO.

Oh, yes there is. There must be. Here.

[*He stoops and picks up a bit of wood hardly
more than six inches long.*]

MARIANGELA.

And you came for this?

LOLLO.

[*With an ambiguous laugh.*]

For this and for something else. It must be there.
[*Pointing to the kitchen- door in the background.*] It's
surely in there.

[*Strides toward the door to open it. Mariangela,
fairly terror-stricken, ashen white, spreads
out her arms and bars his way.*]

MARIANGELA.

What are you looking for? Can't you tell me?

LOLLO.

Certainly. Of course. Why shouldn't I tell you?

MARIANGELA.

[*All aquiver.*]

Tell me what you need. I'll get it for you. I'm your wife, am I not?

LOLLO.

Certainly. You're my wife. Exactly. You go ahead of me with the light. Open that door, now! [*All at once he springs upon her and seizes the light, which she was about to drop.*] Ehi, Mariangela! You want to leave me in the dark — so that I sha'n't find anything?

MARIANGELA.

[*In confusion, stammering.*]

There's so much wood inside there! I'm afraid something might happen if I went in there with a light. Tell me what you need. Perhaps I can get it myself.

LOLLO.

[*After a moment's hesitation.*]

Here. I'm looking for a cord, so that I can tie it to the tip of this bit of wood.

MARIANGELA.

Do you want my apron-strings? Will they do?

LOLLO.

Yes! With a woman's apron-strings you can tie even the devil himself!

[*He puts the lamp back upon the table, leans the gun against the wall, and sits down in the chair nearby, inclined forward, his legs spread apart, his arms hanging between his thighs. He is silent. Mariangela removes her apron and hands it to him; he throws it upon the table beside the wood. In the meantime his wife places before him bread, wine, cheese, and even his pipe filled with tobacco, for she is so upset that she doesn't know what she is doing.*]

What can you be thinking about? Where's your head? One thing at a time, stupid!

[*He takes out his knife from his pocket, opens it, and begins to eat slowly, his back to the wall and his nose pointing downward. From time to time he raises his head and glances toward the kitchen door with a look that his wife follows anxiously.*]

Have you seen Bellama?

MARIANGELA.

[*With a start she drops what she is serving and begins to stammer.*]

No. Why? I haven't seen him.

LOLLO.

[*Grumbles something and pours out wine.*]

MARIANGELA.

Why do you ask? What's Bellama got to do with this?

LOLLO.

[*He wipes his mouth with his hand and looks at her as if he hasn't heard her question, out of lightless eyes that say nothing. He lights his pipe calmly; so calmly that the poor woman gets more and more confused, suddenly falling upon her knees before him to loosen laces of his shoes. He thrusts her back with a kick, muttering:*]

What are you doing now?

MARIANGELA.

I want to dry your feet. You're soaking wet.

LOLLO.

Never mind. I'm going out again.

MARIANGELA.

[*With a sigh of relief.*]

Ah! You've got something to do?

LOLLO.

[*Raising his head and for an instant glaring at her. Then, with an ironic smile.*]

Certainly. I'm going to the feast.

[*He continues to smoke, spitting now and then in any direction.*]

MARIANGELA.

[*Silently clears the table, trembling. All at once she stutters.*]

You talk so queerly this evening. And with such a look!

LOLLO.

I say I've got something to do —with the Musarras. They're waiting for me nearby. We have a wolf to catch tonight.

MARIANGELA.

A wolf?

LOLLO.

Yes. We've been on his trail for so long! I've laid the trap for him. A sure trap. Why, if any fellow is caught in that trap, the devil himself couldn't get him out. And now he's fallen into it! Believe me, I wouldn't want to be in his hide while I'm talking to you now!

MARIANGELA.

[*Instinctively she first casts an anxious glance toward the kitchen door, and then at her husband, who is not even looking at her. He is intent upon his pipe, relishing it, as if already tasting the pleasure of having caught the wolf. There is a crash of thunder — a flash lights up the scene vividly. She crosses herself.*]

What a night, Lord Jesus!

LOLLO.

This is the kind of weather in which all the wicked beasts go prowling about on their evil tricks. But this time the wolf leaves his hide with us. So says your good friend Lollo!

[*A noise is heard suddenly from behind the kitchen door; he seizes his gun.*]

Who's there?

MARIANGELA.

[*More dead than alive.*]

It must be the hens that I shut up in the kitchen — on account of the storm.

LOLLO.

I guess they're scared, too — like you. Look, how pale you are! [*He pours wine for her.*] Have a drop of wine.

MARIANGELA.

No. I haven't the slightest appetite.

LOLLO.

Then I'll drink it.

[*He drinks, then begins to whittle the wood with his pocket-knife, whistling away, blowing, deeply intent upon his work, and tying the apron-string to one end of the stick.*]

MARIANGELA.

[*Feigning deep attention so as to conceal her perturbation; her elbows upon the table, her chin resting upon her palms, she eyes him fixedly, seeking to read his inscrutable countenance.*]

And what's that you're making?

LOLLO.

[*Without looking at her, and continuing to blow and whistle.*]

This? What this is? This is the biscuit that'll close the wolf's mouth. I ought to have another one for you, I ought. Ah! Ah! You're laughing now? The color has come back to your cheeks? You women are like cats; you have nine lives. [*He tugs violently at the apron-string to test its strength.*] Will this snap when he pulls at it with all his might? No. Your string is mighty strong! [*Mariangela continues to stare at him, to discover what he is hiding; she rubs against him, just like a cat, with a palpitating bosom and a pale smile upon her features.*] Steady now, stand still. You'll knock over the lamp. Oil brings misfortune.

MARIANGELA.

[*With an outburst, almost in tears.*]

You bet it brings misfortune! What's the matter with you tonight? Speak, in God's name!

LOLLO.

Nothing the matter with me. Do you see anything wrong?

MARIANGELA.

I see that you have something against me — without any reason!

LOLLO.

Ho, ho! Now you're getting angry! You know everything, you do!

MARIANGELA.

As if I were a child! You tell me a tale about a wolf!

LOLLO.

A tale? You'll see! It's as true as God above!
You'll enjoy it, too, when we've caught him!

MARIANGELA.

Oh! no! Not I!

LOLLO.

Why not? Aren't you my wife?

MARIANGELA.

[*Embarrassed, her eyes moist with tears, about
to take his hand but losing her courage.*]

Yes! Your wife — who loves you so!

LOLLO.

Good. And the harm that's done to me is harm
done to you, too, isn't it?

MARIANGELA.

[*Timidly.*]

You are the master. [*Nodding affirmatively.*] You
are my master!

LOLLO.

Then let me do as I see fit, and have no fear.

MARIANGELA.

It's for you that I fear. I haven't anybody else in
the world!

LOLLO.

Oh, don't worry on my score. I'll take good care
of my hide! A fine thing that would be! To bear
the harm and the jests, too? No, indeed! I've
found friends who are going to lend me a hand.

[*Laughing.*] As a matter of fact, I'm having him caught by their hands. He's a dangerous beast, I'll have you know! He bites when he's cornered! I want to teach him his lesson in my own way, without risking my skin.

MARIANGELA.

What a heart you must have!

LOLLO.

And don't you reckon the bile that's been put into it? [*Whether it is the wine that has loosened his tongue, or whether he finds pleasure in slowly chewing and rechewing the bile that he must have within him — or whether he really wishes to tell his wife the tale of the wolf, so as to quiet her, he continues to chatter like a magpie, scratching his rough chin and almost falling asleep on the chair.*] You want to know how it's done? Listen. You dig a nice deep ditch, hidden beneath dry twigs, and then cover the bed with boughs and leaves and put into the trap a lamb to lure him. The moment he sniffs the fresh flesh he comes tripping gaily along, as if to a wedding. On he comes, his snout in the air! And his eyes sparkle with desire! But once he has crashed into the pitfall he can't so much as touch the lamb, for he has other things to think about.

MARIANGELA.

[*Suspicious, closely scrutinizing his face through her smiling eyes so as to hide her inner commotion, pointing to the stick of wood.*]
And what's that for?

LOLLO.

That's stuck into his mouth so that he can't bite. One of the men lowers it into the hole, and as soon as the wolf has bitten it, another fellow quickly passes the string behind his ears and ties it to the other end of the gag. Then comes the best part of all.

[*The tempest at this point seems about to carry off the hovel. There is a noise in the kitchen. A gust of wind puts out the lamp.*]

MARIANGELA.

[*Screams, adding to the confusion, and stumbles toward the kitchen door.*]

Santa Barbara! Santa Barbara! Wait. I'm looking for some matches. Where are you now?

LOLLO.

[*Who has jumped to the door at the left, with his gun in hand, threateningly.*]

Stand! Quiet, now! Don't move, do you hear? [*He strikes the linch-pin, as green as the match in his hands, and lights the lamp.*] Calm yourself. Calm yourself. Don't make such a racket over nothing.

[*Reaches to the hook for his hood.*]

MARIANGELA.

Are you going?

LOLLO.

You see I am.

The Wolf-Hunt

MARIANGELA.

Will you be back soon?

LOLLO.

Why do you care to know whether I'll be back
early or late?

MARIANGELA.

Like that — to wait for you — to stay up for you.

LOLLO.

No. Go to bed. You were already in bed when
I came.

MARIANGELA.

[*Embarrassed.*]

I?

LOLLO.

You said so yourself. Go back to bed, then, and
commend your soul to God, without fear, for he who
is in the grace of God fears nothing. I can't tell
you whether I'll come back soon or late.

MARIANGELA.

I have done nothing wrong.

LOLLO.

So much the better. Who does no wrong has no
harm to fear.

[*He takes the key out of the table drawer.*]

MARIANGELA.

What? Are you locking me in?

LOLLO.

Yes. So that you won't have to get out of bed again when I return.

MARIANGELA.

[*Nonplussed, throwing her arms around his neck.*]

No! No!

LOLLO.

What does this mean?

MARIANGELA.

[*Pressing fondly against him.*]

Don't leave me! Don't leave me like this! I'm afraid! Better come to bed. It's so cold! Don't you feel it?

LOLLO.

To bed? No. No. Many thanks. First. No! To bed? No! The sleepyhead catches no fish.

MARIANGELA.

Don't you care for me any more? Don't my words mean anything to you any more? Can't you see what a state I'm in?

LOLLO.

Yes, I see. I see. But I must be going now. The Musarras are waiting for me. The father and son, right near here. You know that son of Musarra, whom they all call crazy because his wife ran away from him with Bellamà, Bellamà who plays the rooster with other men's wives. You know him.

MARIANGELA.

[*Confused, stammering.*]

I?

LOLLO.

Yes, you know him. Well, when Bellamà had got all he wanted he left Musarra's wife in the lurch, the poor woman, for she really went crazy! Left her husband, at least, after he has washed his hands in the blood of the seducer. . . .

MARIANGELA.

Lord Jesus! Jesus!

LOLLO.

Ah, Jesus? To have a wife that's everything to a poor man — to cherish her as if she were a child — to give her your very blood and hide to make slippers of, and then see her give herself to the first man that asks for her! But let me go. What do you want?

MARIANGELA.

[*Her hands joined in supplication, her voice broken.*]

Lollo!

LOLLO.

[*Harshly.*]

What do you want? Speak up!

MARIANGELA.

Lollo! Look me straight in the face! [*She sinks to her knees before him and tries to take his hand.*] Let me kiss your hand — as if you were merciful Jesus!

LOLLO.

[*Freeing himself.*]

How tender this evening! You have plenty of tears on tap. Let me be off, I tell you! Out of my way! [*As he opens the door Mariangela tries to escape. He seizes her by the arm and roughly shoves her back into the hut.*] Hey there! Where are you going? You wait for me here!

[*He leaves, locking the door behind him.*]

MARIANGELA.

[*Tearing her hair.*]

Why? What's up? Virgin Mary!

BELLAMA.

[*Pale and uneasy he peers through the kitchen door, then enters on tiptoe, speaking in a lowered voice to Mariangela as he goes by.*]

Good-bye. Good-bye.

MARIANGELA.

[*In raging dismay.*]

Is that how you, too, desert me?

BELLAMA.

[*Trying to open the outer door.*]

Ah, my dear woman! This is no time for tender words! Your husband might come back at any moment! [*Pushing against the door in vain.*] The deuce of a door!

MARIANGELA.

It's locked, from the outside!

BELLAMA.

Oh! This, now!

MARIANGELA.

He's shut us in, under lock and key! He!

BELLAMA.

[*Uneasily.*]

Why? What did he say? I couldn't hear very well from in there.

MARIANGELA.

He said so many things! And with such a look in his eyes! My God!

BELLAMA.

[*At first he tries to act the intrepid hero: he pulls up his trousers, crosses his arms and blusters.*]

Hush! I'm here! Don't be afraid!

[*Then, all at once, whether it is his true nature that has asserted itself, or whether the woman's pacing to and fro like a beast caught in a trap has affected his nerves, he begins to dash madly about, on tiptoe, pallid, his eyes rolling, again trying the door and the iron grating of the window to the right.*]

It's impossible to get out of here. What are we to do now?

MARIANGELA.

I don't know! I don't know! I'm so afraid!

BELLAMA.

[*Running over to her, seizing her by the wrist and shaking her.*]

Afraid? Afraid of whom? Tell me!

MARIANGELA.

Of him! Of my husband! I never saw him in such a mood!

BELLAMA.

Speak! Explain yourself, for the love of God!

MARIANGELA.

[*Dropping into the chair, more dead than alive.*]

Oh, my legs are giving way! I can't stand!

BELLAMA.

[*Furious, forcing her to her feet.*]

And now this! Don't play stupid, I say!

MARIANGELA.

Mariano! My Mariano!

BELLAMA.

[*Shaking her brutally.*]

Speak! Explain yourself! Simpleton!

MARIANGELA.

[*Sinking against the table, and burying her head in her hands.*]

My husband knows everything! He came here on purpose to surprise us.

BELLAMA.

[*Agitated.*]

No. It can't be. Nobody saw me, in the dark.

MARIANGELA.

[*With flaming eyes.*]

I read it in his face. It's absolutely certain. He was searching everywhere, with his gun in his hand!

BELLAMA.

But he didn't find me. And he left without having seen me.

MARIANGELA.

Then why did he lock me in?

BELLAMA.

[*Again becoming uneasy.*]

Yes, why? [*Trying to revive his courage, repeats.*] But then, why did he leave?

MARIANGELA.

He said they were waiting for him. That they're hunting the wolf tonight.

BELLAMA.

Wolf-hunting? That's excellent. Then where do I come in?

MARIANGELA.

One moment he said one thing, the next moment he said another. He spoke with such evil foreboding. And then he locked us in!

BELLAMA.

[*Looking about anxiously, as if seeking an avenue of escape.*]

The devil! That's so!

MARIANGELA.

He's shut us in like a wolf in a trap. Then when he gets back . . .

BELLAMA.

[*Breathlessly.*]

When he gets back? When does he get back?

MARIANGELA.

I don't know. He wouldn't tell me.

BELLAMA.

You never know anything, you!

MARIANGELA.

When he gets back, he'll give us a merry dance!

BELLAMA.

Eh?

MARIANGELA.

[*Tearing her hair.*]

We've got death hanging over our heads, you and I!

BELLAMA.

Don't harp on that, I tell you!

MARIANGELA.

[*Embracing him, weeping.*]

Mariano! My Mariano! I've only you in the world!

BELLAMA.

Yes, but let me go now!

MARIANGELA.

You'll defend me! You've said so many times that you'd do anything for your Mariangela!

BELLAMA.

I haven't even a pen-knife with me.

MARIANGELA.

[*Her face in her apron, crying.*]

Do you see what I've done for you?

BELLAMA.

You've got me into a fine fix, that's what you've done!

MARIANGELA.

I? I?

BELLAMA.

Who else, then? Enough. Let's lose no time in prattle. Better let us find a way out of this. Perhaps they really are out wolf-hunting. If that's the case, then we have time until tomorrow.

MARIANGELA.

I hope to God it's so! May the sainted souls avail us!

BELLAMA.

[*Likewise somewhat encouraged.*]

Don't be afraid, I told you! I'm here!

MARIANGELA.

But he'll come with the Musarras! They're on
the wolf-hunt, too.

BELLAMA.

[*Terrified.*]

Eh? Who was that you said? Eh?

MARIANGELA.

Yes, the Musarras, father and son.

> [*Bellama, without further heed, makes a mad
> dash for escape. All at once, as if struck by
> an idea, he places a chair upon the bed and
> prepares to clamber up.*

BELLAMA.

Up there. . . . If I can only reach it! If I can
only get to the roof! I'll smash in the tiles, as true
as God! Here, hold this chair for me, will you?

MARIANGELA.

And how about me?

BELLAMA.

[*Standing on the bed, greatly excited.*]

Your husband can make *you* swallow that tale
about the wolf, for you're a goose!

MARIANGELA.

And how about me? . . . when my husband sees
that you've escaped through the roof?

BELLAMA.

[*Making desperate efforts to reach the roof.*]

He's got together with the Musarras because *they've* got a grudge against me, too!

MARIANGELA.

[*In exasperation.*]

I know all about it! Because of Neli Musarra's wife. . . . You wretch, you!

BELLAMA

[*Agitated.*]

Much I care about Musarra's wife now! . . . And a fine moment this is to make a jealous scene!

MARIANGELA.

[*Now likewise highly excited.*]

All you think of is your own skin!

BELLAMA.

[*Furious.*]

Of my own skin! Yes I do, my fine lady! You've landed me in a trap!

MARIANGELA.

[*Tugging at his leg.*]

And you're deserting me . . . leaving me all alone . . . with death staring me in the face!

BELLAMA.

[*Kicking her away.*]

Let go of me, curse you!

MARIANGELA.

[*Exasperated, kicking the chair from under him.*]

Curse *you!* A curse on you forever, for you've ruined me!

BELLAMA.

[*Furious, brandishing the chair over her head.*]

I'll finish you! As true as God, I'll finish you before your husband does!

MARIANGELA.

Would that I'd been stricken before you ever came into my life! Would that some malignant fever had consumed me!

BELLAMA.

It would have been far better!

MARIANGELA.

It's all your fault! You've ruined me, just as you ruined Musarra's wife, you scoundrel!

BELLAMA.

So now you're throwing Musarra's wife up to me, are you? You didn't talk like that when you were chasing after me and begging me to leave her, did you? I guess not!

MARIANGELA.

I, chasing after you? You miserable wretch!

BELLAMA.

You shameless liar! You'd stand by the door and smile at me! You, with a husband that was too

good for you, swapping him for the first man that
passed by!

MARIANGELA.

[*As she hears the turn of the key in the outside
door, she begins to scream.*]

Help! Help!

BELLAMA.

[*Seizing her by the throat.*]

Shut up, damn you! I'll strangle you!

MARIANGELA.

[*Struggling, biting his hands.*]

Help! Help!

BELLAMA.

[*Hearing the door open he rushes, cursing, into
the room at the rear.*]

A curse on you! Damn you!

MARIANGELA.

[*To her husband, as he appears on the threshold,
on guard, his gun in position to fire.*]

Help! There's a man here! . . . Inside there!
. . . While I was undressing!

LOLLO.

[*Calling to the Musarras outside.*]

Musarra! Friend Neli! Here's the fellow you're
looking for!

CURTAIN.

ERCOLE LUIGI MORSELLI

(1882–1921)

The short life of Morselli was as checkered as it could be made by a youthful thirst for adventure, a goading poverty and an underlying spiritual unrest. Born at Pesaro, he was early taken by his parents to Modena, and soon thence to Florence. Here he finished the courses given at the elementary schools and advanced to the university, where for two years he devoted himself to the study of medicine and letters. He took no degree, but his intercourse with such minds as Papini and Prezzolini helped to sharpen his wits, and later, when he needed a little friendly notice, Papini beat the drum for him with those short, staccato thumps for which he is noted — or was noted, before the astounding conversion that is signalized in his recent book, "Storia di Cristo." To Papini, indeed, Morselli owes not a little for his crossing of the Italian border and for exaltation as a writer of modern tragedy that lifts him clearly above both d'Annunzio and Sem Benelli.

According to the evidence available, Morselli's life at Florence was a strange admixture of ardent study and wild debauch. In his twentieth year, in company of his friend, Valerio Ratti, he suddenly launched upon a sea voyage, and before he returned to Florence he had wandered from Capetown to Buenos Aires, to Cornwall, to London, to Paris, earning his living now by his pen, now by the most cheeky imposture. At Buenos Aires he had even enlisted to fight against Saravia's army of Blancos in the war with Uruguay, but it does not appear that any blood was shed and Saravia's death soon brought about peace. Once back in Italy — "the most penitent and happy of prodigal sons" — Morselli founded a large commercial and industrial review called *Mercurio*, which ran for no less than five years and died of — honesty. In order to marry he was compelled to borrow 150 *lire* to proceed with the ceremony; this was but the beginning of straits that often brought him to the pangs of hunger. His mind reverted to writing, at which in the early days he had managed to turn a penny, and the result was that peculiar little book called "Favole per i re d'oggi" (Fables for the Kings of Today). The encouraging reception it was accorded resulted in the composition of the one-act play "Acqua sul fuoco," which is included in this collection. The affecting little piece, however, made very little impression at the time, and Morselli returned to Pesaro in the dreary conviction that he had not been cut out for a dramatist. His next refuge was poetry, and he set about the writing of "Orione," his first tragedy, which is poetic not in the narrow sense of rhymes and meters, but in the ampler one of outlook, atmosphere and implication. Originally produced in 1910, it made the tour of Milan, Trieste, Modena and Florence.

The author, who was encountering plenty of opposition among his fellow-craftsmen, was accused of classicism, and perhaps to refute the charge, wrote the modern play "La Prigione" (The Prison), which Tina di Lorenzo acted in Milan, Turin, Florence and even South America. Close upon "The Prison" followed the other one-act play here included, "Il Domatore Gastone," which ran for ten nights in Rome.

Soon we discover Morselli in the "movies" as an actor, and he readily advances to the position of a director. The war, however, cuts short his cinematographic ventures. His great tragedy "Glauco" is now beginning to take shape; he reads the first draught to the composer Franchetti, who is so struck with it that immediately he acquires the rights to set it to music. A period of illness intervenes, and it is not until he is out of the sanatorium that Morselli writes the final draught in twenty days, at Blevio. He leaves the sole copy in the compartment of a railroad car and it is recovered only after a campaign of telephone calls and telegrams. From one manager to another it travels, until at last it is produced through the enterprise of Virgilio Talli and acted in triumph by Annibale Betrone, proving to be the greatest success since Benelli's "La cena delle beffe" (The Supper of Jests). The furore created by "Glauco" led to the republication of Morselli's other labors; he had already been working upon two tragedies, "Dafne e Cloe" and "Belfagor"; now he considered a new modern play in three acts, to be named "L'Incontro." In 1919 he was awarded the government prize of 6000 *lire* for "Glauco," and his future seemed assured. Declining health, however, led to his early death from tuberculosis of the lungs.

Morselli's fiction comprises the "Favole per i re d'oggi," "Storie da ridere . . . e da piangere" (Tales for laughter . . . and tears), and "Il trio Stefania." The fables are filled with cynicism, irony, recognition of human vanity, bantering mockery. Beneath the sneers is a spirit of tolerance, and a withdrawal that enables the author to consider his fellowmen as if he were a god endowed with a sense of humor and of human frailties. The tales for laughter and for tears are not divided into those meant for pleasure and those written to agitate the emotions. The title, I imagine, signifies that each tale contains both elements in a very human blend, even as does life itself. As the writer declares in that strange tale "Italien, Liebe, Blut! — a German novel left halfcompleted through my good offices," in which Boccaccesque moments alternate with Heinesque moods, " . . . I was made that way: I would laugh and laugh, yet at bottom I took everything seriously, even as now, when I no longer laugh."

The man is fundamentally ironic and symbolic in his outlook upon life. This does not have to be read into his lines; it is there, in body and in spirit. No doubt plays like his two tragedies lend themselves to the sort of symbol-reading that made the perusal of Ibsen's critics so hilariously interesting when the

great Norwegian dawned upon us some fifteen years
ago. Perhaps this sort of literary palm-reading will
never go out of fashion. But when one reads Morselli
for exactly what the text says, without thinking of
the man's career and without attempting to read
meanings between the lines and into the phrases, one
realizes that one is in the presence of an ironic
spirit, a cynical soul gifted with symbolical insinuation. The Italian's humor is the kind that vibrates
with overtones of a mockery that does not spare
himself; his beauty is not the mere sound of words
and the music of phrase; it is instinct with connota-
tions of man's smallness in the eyes of nature and of
fate.

I need not indicate the symbolic elements in the
one-act plays, which are here for the reader to enjoy.
Even the modern play "La Prigione" is symbolic
from the very title, which signifies the mental torture
of sustaining a family-lie, of "putting on a front."
It is written somewhat in the vein of Giacosa, but
tinted throughout with the author's characteristic
methods. As to "Orione" and "Glauco," the first,
written about ten years earlier than the second, is not
so good because of its diffuseness and because it
carries less poetic conviction. The symbolism is less
effective, and while the action is excellent in scenes
it is neither so cumulative nor so climatic as in the
later play. Orione, the god, is less impressive than
Glauco, the seeker, and Merope is less colorful than
Glauco's sweetheart, Scilla. In "Glauco," Morselli's
diction, purged of merely rhetorical ornament and

free of self-conscious grandiloquence, attains a
memorable simplicity that parallels the admirably
luminous simplicity of the action. The symbolism,
too, is such that it adds to the humanness of the
characters rather than converts them into the terms
of a dramatic equation. Some Italian critics have
objected to the symbolic interpretation of these
two plays in particular. Yet surely, even considering
the tragedies in the strictest manner that so exacting
a philosopher as Benedetto Croce would require, one
is justified in extracting the symbols that the author
has unmistakably put into them. And so considered,
"Orione" portrays man's helpless position in the face
of nature's laws, even as "Glauco" suggests man's
tardy recognition that glory is less than love.
"Qualunque vita è abietta si è fatta al solo scopo di
vivere! . . . e qualunque vita è santa se un fine
l'illumina! . . ." exclaims Jacopo in "La Prigione."
"Any life is abject if it be concerned only with living,
and any life is holy if a purpose illumine it." We
have Morselli's own word for it that he aimed to
create a little beauty through his writings, and his
interpretation of the word "purpose" by no means
signifies an art marred by the obtrusion of moral
preachment.

Morselli's position in the contemporary letters of
his country is a considerable one, and already secure.
The triumphant reception of "Glauco" by a national
audience trained in the best traditions of the poetic
drama led more than one critic to behold in the
young playwright the precursor of a new, peculiarly

modern, poetic tragedy. Amidst the ruck of fantastic productions that infested the "grotesque" theatre, with its plays labelled "visions," "confessions," "parables" — anything, indeed, but drama or comedy—Morselli developed an idiom and an atmosphere all his own. His early death was a serious blow to the Italian stage, for with D'Annunzio's heroics and Benelli's recent reversion to prose and apostolic mysticism, Italy needs more than ever the unpretentious beauty, the pure line and the harmonious colors that Morselli would have added to its store.

PERSONS

BISTONE,	*a shepherd*
RIGA,	*his wife*
OLIVA,	*their daughter*
GIGI,	*their son*
LEOPOLDO,	*a sailor*
PIPPO,	*a young charcoal burner*
DENTE DI LEGNO,	*an old charcoal burner*

WATER UPON FIRE

SCENE: *The interior of a shepherd's hut in the Tuscan Apennines. To the left, a fireplace in which logs are burning, and before it, a very rough table upon which stands an oil lamp. At the rear, left, is the sink with a grated window above it. In the middle background, the door; to the right, close to the back wall, a pallet stretched upon the floor; above this hangs a black coat, and near by a tiny table on which is placed a little basket of unfinished willow work. The wall to the right is a rustic, wooden partition, with a doorway. The ceiling is formed by the rafters of a roof that inclines toward the door at the back.*

At the rise of the curtain the neighboring mountain tops may be seen through the open door, glowing in the sunset. Gigi is fast asleep, stretched out upon the pallet; Riga is paring some boiled, steaming potatoes, and blowing upon her fingers with the noise of a bellows.

RIGA.

[*As Bistone comes in.*]

Here he is again!

BISTONE.

No use talking! That goat doesn't look well to me at all.

Riga.

[*Angrily.*]

What do you imagine ails it now? Every little while . . .

Bistone.

Here are you butting in . . . you know everything! If you'd only hurry along with those potatoes! I know a thing or two about animals, don't I? When I tell you that she'll not be alive by tomorrow . . . don't make any mistake . . . it's as true as if Christ himself had spoken it! No use talking!

Riga.

Blasphemy! May Christ pardon you! A fine head you imagine you've got! Who can ever know what you've got inside of it?

Bistone.

Now then! Those potatoes . . . they're for this evening! No use talking.

Riga.

There he goes with his "no use talking"! Shut up, won't you, and you'll talk less nonsense! Better wait till Oliva comes back, and show her the goat. Now *she* really understands a thing or two. And she has a way of curing those creatures . . . Not like you, who kill them if you lay a finger upon their bodies!

Bistone.

Now what was I saying? Chatterbox! Suppose you keep quiet for a monent! I was just about to say that I wanted my supper right away, so that when Oliva comes back with the sheep, I can send Gigi to lock them in for the night and take her along with me to have a look at the goat.

RIGA.

Excellent!

BISTONE.

Doesn't that suit you, either?

RIGA.

And Oliva go without her supper, the poor darling? She's had nothing since her slice of cheese this morning! When *you* come back from watching the sheep there's no reason in you. You want to eat at once! . . . And God help us if the supper's not ready!

BISTONE.

Eh! . . . eh! . . . And now tell me that I'm not fond of the girl! . . .

RIGA.

No, I didn't mean that . . . but . . .

BISTONE.

"But" what? . . . "But" what? . . . When one of the creatures is dying, it seems to me a body can eat a half hour later. Isn't that so? . . .

[*The tinkling of a bell is heard more and more clearly — such a bell as the coalmen are wont to hang from the neck of the first donkey in their little black caravan.*

PIPPO.

[*Looking in through the doorway.*]

Howd'do, folks!

RIGA.

[*Very affably.*]

Good evening, Pippo!

BISTONE.

How's the weather?

PIPPO.

Bad! . . . The whole Poggio Orsaia has become sullen, and in a little while it'll be pouring! . . . A regular cloudburst! Let me have my coat, Riga! . . . I guess this time we can really say good-bye to summer! [*Going out to the donkeys.*] Whoa, there!

[*The tinkling of the bell suddenly ceases.*]

RIGA.

[*To Pippo as he returns.*]

Here's your coat . . . I sewed on that missing button. [*She goes out, looks at the sky and the surrounding landscape.*] But where's that ninny Oliva?

PIPPO.

[*Places his switch upon the table and puts on his coat.*]

BISTONE.

Eh! She must have gone toward la Cocca. I told her to! That's where you find such a fine big shade; the animals like it far better than Tre Faggi.

PIPPO.

The rascal! . . . So it was you? . . . I thought
so . . . way up la Cocca! . . . I called her so
long! . . . Bah! As if I were calling the moon!
. . . Let me relight my pipe.

[*Goes to the fireplace, bends over the fire and
lights his pipe.*]

RIGA.

[*Who, in the meantime, has shut the window.*]
The wretch! [*Noticing Pippo bent over the fire.*]
Couldn't you have asked me? I'd have lighted it for
you without you going and soiling that handsome
cloak.

PIPPO.

Eh! . . . [*Shaking himself.*] Only ashes! Good
evening, folks. [*He pauses upon the threshold. The
wind blows strongly. The first drops begin to fall.*] To' !
Here's the rain! Good-bye, pipe! [*He raps his pipe
against the jamb of the door, then slowly puts it into the
cloak pocket.*] I had a chestnut stick . . .

[*Goes toward the table.*]

RIGA.

[*Suddenly takes the stick from the table.*]
Here it is, Pippo.

PIPPO.

[*Takes his stick. As he walks toward the door,
he notices Gigi, who, eyes still closed, is
turning around on the pallet. He strikes
Gigi playfully, but fairly hard, and shouts.*]

Hey, there! When does day start for you?

[*Goes out and stops once more, while Gigi, closing his eyes again, stretches and mutters unintelligible words in reply to Pippo's friendly greeting.*]

RIGA.

Hit him harder! . . . Are you leaving, Pippo? . . .

PIPPO.

Yes, I'm going away . . . Give Oliva my regards when she returns! [*Turns back a step, without entering the hut.*] By the way! I haven't any loads for my donkeys on Sunday! . . . I'll take you to mass: you and Oliva! . . . Tell Oliva to be sure and be at home . . . If not, I'll get angry! [*He leaves, almost running in his heavy boots.*] Regards to everybody. Whoa, there! . . .

RIGA.

[*As the bell's tinkling grows less and less distinct, she waves good-bye to Pippo from the doorway. Then she shuts the door without locking it; the water makes the door creak.*

Good-by-y-y-ye! [*To Gigi, impetuously.*] A fine figure of a simpleton you are! You disgust everybody! . . . Always on that cursed filthy pallet! . . . I'll throw it into the ditch on you some fine day. [*To Bistone.*] Well, then. Cut the bread. [*She gives him the bread and the knife, and Bistone slices it.*] Oh, [*to Gigi again*] I'm talking to *you*, Gigi! Wild cat there, get up, in the Lord's name! I can't recall

how tall you are! Won't you get up even for the
potatoes?

GIGI.

[*Finally stirs.*]

Hm! So you, too, listen to what that black snout
of a Pippo says! Fetch me the potatoes, mamma
. . . and better keep an eye on Oliva so that she
doesn't come to a bad end with that firebrand!

RIGA.

You must have had some terrible nightmare!
May the good Lord make you see the light some day.
I only hope that Oliva would take a liking to Pippo!
. . . [*As she speaks, she places a plate of salad and
potatoes before Bistone, who falls at once to eating.*]
He's what I call a man; not one of you contemptible
shepherds! Do you see how much money he makes
with those black sacks of his? I only hope that
simpleton of an Oliva will have him! Who can
tell what she's mooning about, that girl? Some
prince, no doubt! . . . All on account of those foolish
fables I used to tell her when she was a child! She
must be dreaming about her Prince Charming with a
golden helmet, mounted upon a black steed with a
silver saddle . . . who had heard of a beautiful
shepherdess . . . more beautiful than the queen
. . . and then set about seeking her amidst these
sooty hovels . . . and when he has found her, he
carries her off and shuts her up in . . .

GIGI.

Fetch me my potatoes, mamma, or I'll go to sleep again!

RIGA.

Sleep? You cabbage-stalk! Here's your potatoes! Didn't you hear what father said just now? You must lock up the sheep tonight.

LEOPOLDO.

          [Outside, knocking on the door.]

May I come in?

BISTONE.

          [Through a mouth crammed with food.]

Come in.

RIGA.

          [Turning to her husband, in a low voice.]

Who is it?

BISTONE.

Who do you think? Somebody on his way! *[Aloud.]* Come in!

LEOPOLDO.

    [Enters. He wears a heavy, dark blue jacket and a Basque cap. Those who have seen his kind at once recognize a sailor from the large merchant vessels. He is about thirty; the sea, the sun, the wind have engraved a few deep wrinkles upon his countenance, rendering it more solid, more handsome.

Good evening, shepherds! *[He shakes the water off him and goes to hang his cap upon a chair near the*

fireplace, saying] May I? For a downpour like this
I should have had my oilskin along!

BISTONE.

You're a stranger, eh? Won't you sit down and
have something with us? . . . But no, first . . .
take off that jacket. It's soaking wet. I'll get you a
dry one . . . a bit ripped, of course . . . the best
that we poor shepherd folk can afford . . . but it's
dry!

LEOPOLDO.

No, no, thanks! Don't disturb yourself.

BISTONE.

You'll do well to change . . . Take my advice.
No use talking, when . . .

LEOPOLDO.

Let me have my way; never fear. My shoulders
are well accustomed to the weather! I'd far rather
take off these shoes for a moment; I bought them
specially for tramping over these mountains. They
must be made of elephant hide! Ah, that's better!
. . . I'm too used to feeling my feet free!

GIGI.

[*Looks at the newcomer with diffident indifference, and crunches his potatoes.*

RIGA.

[*Examines the stranger closely, with great difficulty holding back the questions that come to her lips. She seems not very well disposed toward him.*

LEOPOLDO.

[*With his naturally swift movements he has taken from his valise a pair of Spanish* ZAPATILLAS *and has exchanged them for his coarse, mountaineers' boots. He strides downstage from the fireplace with satisfied gait.*

BISTONE.

To' ! There's a lively chap for you! . . . By Diana! How quick you are! I wish you could teach a little of that to my son there!

[*Points to Gigi.*]

RIGA.

[*Coming to a resolution.*]

But . . . here . . . in a manner of speaking . . . How under the sun did you ever land up in these parts? . . . You could have been so comfortable in the city!

BISTONE.

[*Shouting.*]

And what business is that of yours, busybody? [*To Leopoldo*]. Don't say a word. Understand? Not a breath! . . . For I don't care to know a thing! . . . No use talking! . . . Take a seat here right away [*strikes the table with his palm*] and have a bite. Afterwards, if it please you to talk, you'll tell us who you are, so that we may remember you. Understand? [*To Riga, irritated.*] Since when, in this humble cabin of mine, has any one ever asked "Who are you?" of a Christian who comes for shelter? The longer a man lives, the more he learns of a woman's queer ways! Give him a slice of cheese, Riga . . . the cheese we started yesterday! [*Riga, with ill grace, does as she is bidden.*] Here you are, and welcome . . . Shepherd folks' food . . . No use talking . . . My dear sir . . . How shall I call you?

LEOPOLDO.

Leopoldo.

BISTONE.

My dear Signor Leopoldo! . . . Just taste a bit of our mountaineers' fare!

LEOPOLDO.

If we only could have it always at sea! When we're ashore we see to it that we eat like lords, sure enough! But at sea . . . ! You wouldn't eat what we have to take sometimes!

> [*Riga, seated in a corner of the fireplace, cocks her ear. — Gigi has finished his potatoes and bread, and placing the plate upon the floor resumes his sleeping posture. Leopoldo extracts from his pocket a Catalonian knife that glistens like a mirror; he opens it, and Bistone and Riga are stricken with admira-*

*tion for its three springs. Riga's amazement
is compounded of fear and mistrust.*]

BISTONE.

A fine instrument!

LEOPOLDO.

Fine, eh? . . . I bought this in America. Did you
ever hear of America?

BISTONE.

All of eighteen years ago. I had just been married.
One day a fellow came up this way and told a heap
of tales. . . You should have heard him! . . .

LEOPOLDO.

He wanted to take you to America, too, didn't
he?

BISTONE.

Sure enough! How do you know? . . .

LEOPOLDO.

My good man! You don't have to be a magician to
guess that! There must be hundreds like him scour-
ing all Italy in search of laborers to take back to
America! But why didn't you go? . . . It's a great
country! You who live on sheep . . . There's a
kind of sheep yonder that has tails so long and thick
that they have to be tied to the animals' crupper!
I've seen some fine specimens . . . The tail alone
weighed eight kilos! . . .

BISTONE AND RIGA.

[Together.]

Oo-o-o-ooh!

[Gigi begins to snore.]

LEOPOLDO.

Upon my word! As far as I'm concerned, to tell the truth, I'm indifferent . . . But you! . . . Who can say how delighted you would have been! We sailors are too used to seeing a world of wonderful things. There's nothing now that can take us by surprise . . . except beautiful maidens!

BISTONE.

[Without enthusiasm, and even with a slight trace of instinctive hostility.]

So you're a man of the sea, are you? One of those who sails in the ships . . . and goes all around the world . . . and carry goods . . . I see, now . . . I see! And how does it happen that you come up here to visit us shepherd folk, who are born and die inside a tiny cabin? *[From the distance comes the sound of a sheep bell. He turns at once to Riga.]* Do you hear the bell, Riga? *[Then to Gigi.]* Gigi, by Diana! What did I tell you before? Go and lock up the sheep and call Oliva . . . Tell her to come here at once. *[With an effort, Gigi rises and leaves, adjusting his sash around his waist. — To Gigi.]* Oh, and see to it that "la Rossaccia" is there. Don't do as you did this past Saturday . . . *[As if to himself.]* With all this fine talk I'd half forgotten about the little goat.

[*Gigi has left the door open. The rain has ceased. The sky, covered with dark clouds, has hastened night.*]

LEOPOLDO.

Is this Oliva a daughter of yours?

BISTONE.

[*Nods affirmatively.*]

GIGI.

[*Outside.*]

Oliva-a-a-a-a! . . .

LEOPOLDO.

A pretty name!

OLIVA.

[*Outside, from a distance.*]

E-e-e-e-h! . . .

GIGI.

[*Outside, as he returns.*]

Come ho-o-o-o-ome! . . . I'm locking up the sheep toni-i-i-i-ight! . . .

LEOPOLDO.

And who can tell how many children you have! You shepherds economize on everything . . . except that!

BISTONE.

No, no. I haven't so many! Only six of them living.

RIGA.

[*Inquisitive.*]

And you? Have you any children?

[*Oliva enters, almost running and somewhat out of breath. She has heard her mother's question, and turns her eyes to see to whom it is addressed. She hears the reply which comes instantly, but distractedly, from Leopoldo, whose eyes are fixed upon Oliva's beautiful face and shapely person.*

LEOPOLDO.

I? No, no, no! Free as a fish! [*Then, with sailor-like gallantry.*] Good evening, Oliva! . . .

OLIVA.

[*In surprise, she eyes Leopoldo from top to toe, then blushing all over she lowers her glance and murmurs.*]

Happy evening.

RIGA.

Father wants to take you to see la Monica. He says she's ill. But you must eat first.

OLIVA.

La Monica ill? I must go to her at once. . . . What's the matter with her, father?

BISTONE.

[*To Riga.*]

There! See? . . . She has more sense than you!

RIGA.

And such sense . . . Oliva's got to eat now. I must have my way sometimes! [*To Oliva.*] And you listen to what he says, ninny! Can't you see that

if we'd have believed him all the time those three
little goats would have died ten times over . . .
Once it was la Calzetta Nera who couldn't swallow
any more; another time, la Rosa was certain to
die while giving birth. Remember, Oliva? Still
another. . . .

BISTONE.

That's right! . . . A fine time for your long
speeches! . . . Listen to me, Oliva. Your Monica is
a goner for sure! No use talking! . . .

OLIVA.

Be good, father! You run to her in the meantime.
I'll satisfy mamma. I'll eat a bite and then come
right away. All right?

BISTONE.

Uhm! . . .

> [*He goes out grumbling. Oliva takes a slice of
> bread from the table and begins chewing it
> without sitting down before Bistone's place,
> where Riga has put the plate of potato salad.
> She seems agitated, intimidated, but also
> fairly drawn by the glance of the guest, who,
> since her arrival, has not ceased for an
> instant to stare at her.*]

RIGA.

So much the better . . . He's gone!

> [*She sets to work polishing some milk buckets
> with ashes from the hearth. — Pause.*]

LEOPOLDO.

[Breaks the silence with a tender voice that does not seem to be his own.]

Why don't you have a seat, beautiful Oliva? Are you afraid of the sailor man? . . . The sailor man has a hard skin, but a soft heart! . . .

OLIVA.

Thanks.

[Timidly she approaches the table, but does not take a seat. At the word "sailor" a slight gesture of admiration escapes her.]

LEOPOLDO.

You're in a hurry to see your little goat . . . eh? You are so fond of them, aren't you? . . . of those little creatures of yours!

OLIVA.

I'm a shepherdess! After mother and father, they are closest to my heart . . . I don't suppose you're over fond of them. . .

LEOPOLDO.

And you, just tell me — are you fond of the sea? . . .

OLIVA.

I? . . . Why . . . but first I should like to know whether a certain thing is true . . . Can you read?

LEOPOLDO.

Yes.

OLIVA.

Then . . . [*louder*] Mother, give him Memmo's
letter. [*To Leopoldo.*] That's my brother, who's a
soldier. They've just sent him to such a far country!
Perhaps you've been there? Ge . . . Genoa. . .

LEOPOLDO.

Eh! Genoa! The deuce! To us sailors that's as
familiar and homelike a place as your hut to you
shepherds!

> [*During a pause, until Riga returns from the
> adjoining room with the letter, he gazes
> fixedly at Oliva.*]

RIGA.

Poor Memmo. There was a real son for you. Not
the scamp you saw there. [*Points to the pallet.*]
Couldn't they have taken this one? . . . I don't
know what to do with him! No. They had to take
just that one and no other.

OLIVA.

Console yourself, mother! Only five months more.
. . . They'll pass quickly enough.

RIGA.

Here. [*Kisses the letter, hands it to Leopoldo, and
then, to herself.*] If he'd only write again at once!

OLIVA.

See if you can find the place where he speaks of the
sea. . . It must be after. . .

Water Upon Fire

LEOPOLDO.

[Reading with effort.]

Here it is, if I'm not mistaken: "At last, after having heard so much talk of it, I've seen the ocean with my own eyes. What a meadow that would make if God had created it of earth instead of water. How can I ever make you understand it all, Oliva?"

OLIVA.

How big is the ocean?

LEOPOLDO.

My dear girl! You could travel for months and months over it, without ever seeing land in any direction! And then the ocean is deep . . . how can I explain it? . . . If you took all these mountains of yours, and threw them in, not even a tree top would be left sticking out of the water. Can you imagine that? . . .

OLIVA.

Poor little me! It gets me crazy to think of it! . . . Read a little more . . . I do so like to hear you read . . .

LEOPOLDO.

Yes? . . . Imagine that, now! . . . "A friend of mine, a sailor, just married a good-looking girl who's the daughter of a fisherman. What a celebration! they invited me and I certainly had a great time! . . . But then, think of a sailor's life! After a single month of wedded life, he sets sail and is away for a year!"

OLIVA.

But can that be true? . . . You tell me! . . .

LEOPOLDO.

Of course! That's the kind of life we lead, my
dear little girl. It's all a saying good-bye from the
time you're born till you die! . . . Those who love
us must be forever weeping! . . . You, Oliva —
you wouldn't marry a sailor, would you? . . .

OLIVA.

[*Hesitating.*]

Weeping is no sin.

LEOPOLDO.

Well said! But suppose you were to choose
between a shepherd who comes home every evening
. . . and a sailor who goes away and is never sure
of returning. And he goes so far away that you read
his letters a month after they were written . . .
And even if he writes, "I am well, and have had a
fine voyage!" you're unable to smile, because even
as you read . . . he may be the prey of some shark!

OLIVA.

[*Becoming serious and almost offended at these
last words.*]

Don't say such horrid things! . . . Read just a
tiny bit more, rather . . . Does he say anything else
about the ocean?

LEOPOLDO.

[Glancing through the letter.]

Here . . . "And how these fellows do love the
sea! We men of the mountain aren't very much in
their eyes! *[He laughs.]* They'd wish to have all the
world one big ocean! But I say to myself: then what
would become of our little creatures? Where would
they find pasture?"

OLIVA.

There! You see, it's true that you're not fond of
sheep! . . .

LEOPOLDO.

That's because we have our own sheep! . . . If
you could only see them, Oliva! . . When the
fresh breeze rises, they swarm over the sea's great
plain. . . . They're whiter than yours, and there's
millions of them. . . . And no one watches over
them, for they all flock together. . . They have
no master, nobody knows whence they come nor
whither they're bound, they don't let themselves
be shorn, nor even milked . . . But they're so
beautiful . . . so free . . . yonder . . . upon the
water! If you could only see them, Oliva . . .

OLIVA.

What kind of sheep can they be?

LEOPOLDO.

They're made of white foam, Oliva! And the wind
creates them, and they dash and leap over the
waves! . . . Sometimes, when I'm not on watch,

instead of sleeping I gaze at them, leaning like this
[*he rests his elbows upon the table and presses his fists
against his temples*] against the gunwale for an hour
at a time! . . .

Oliva.

Then do as I do! . . . When I sit on the hill top
and watch over my poor little darlings . . . who
walk hither and thither so softly . . . and turn
about me . . . browsing among the rocks, and
gazing at me every other moment out of those clear
little eyes . . . There's no danger of my growing
weary under that sun! . . . And all you hear is a
wasp buzzing through the air . . . Eh! If you were
to stay a little while yonder on that hill, you'd learn
to love those little darlings of mine. . . .

Leopoldo.

Eh! . . . If I were there . . . Oliva! . . . **it**
would be far easier for me to learn to love you! . . .
>   [*While this conversation has been going on,
>   Riga has twice gone into and returned from
>   the adjoining room where her little ones are
>   abed. Twice she has resumed her hard
>   chores, when anew comes the sounds of an
>   infant's whimpering.*]

Riga.

Go see what's ailing Settimo, will you, Oliva? He
won't give me a moment's rest this evening. . .

Oliva.

[Rudely waked from a beautiful vision into which Leopoldo's words had lulled her. She hardly understands her mother's words, then, with a short exclamation runs into the room.]

Riga.

[Leaving her work for a moment and turning to Leopoldo.]

Now you'll tell me, won't you, Signor Leopoldo? Whatever put it into your head to climb up into these mountains? I didn't want to offend you before . . . You understood! . . . That blockhead of a Bistone doesn't know what he's about . . . Was there anything wrong in my asking? . . .

Leopoldo.

Wrong? The deuce! I'll tell you right away: I accompanied a friend of mine, poor devil . . . One of those friends whose like can never be found! *[Very sad.]*

Riga.

What happened to him? . . . Dead? . . .

Leopoldo.

No . . . But to me it's the same as if he had died! He married a country girl: a certain Virginia . . . from Rifiglio . . . Perhaps you know her? . . .

Riga.

[Pauses for a moment, then shakes her head.]

LEOPOLDO.

A beautiful blonde . . . Enough said! He fell
in love with her one day in Florence. They went
out together and from that day on he has had eyes
for nothing else! . . . But she didn't want to
marry a sailor. . . and he — nobody could stop
him—looked about until he found a job in a factory.
And yesterday they were married! . . .

RIGA.

You don't say!

OLIVA.

[*After having heard Leopoldo's tale from behind
the partition door, unseen.*]

You'd better go to him, mamma. He pays no
attention to me . . . Hear him?

RIGA.

Benedetto! . . . What can be the matter with
him this evening? Someone must have cast an evil
eye upon him! . . .

LEOPOLDO.

But *such* an evil eye! . . . [*Looking upon Oliva
with desire, and happy to be left for a moment alone
with her.*] He wants his mother. . . that's easily
understood!

RIGA.

[*Goes into the next room ill-humoredly.
Oliva returns to her former position, and
remains standing. The mesh of dreams in
which she has been caught weaves all around*

her soul. She stares fixedly at the floor, following some happy fancy of hers.]

LEOPOLDO.

[*After a brief silence.*]

What are you thinking of, Oliva?

RIGA.

[*Singing in the next room.*]

" I saw a siren in mid-ocean
Upon a reef, and she was weeping, weeping."

OLIVA.

I was thinking that there are some happy persons
in the world! . . .

RIGA.

[*As above.*]

" I've seen so many fishes cry
At the sad words she said!"

LEOPOLDO.

How beautiful you are, Oliva! Perhaps . . . who
knows . . . if you loved me, I, too, might be happy!
[*Arises and approaches her from behind, glancing
furtively toward the partition door and the door at the
rear.*]

RIGA.

[*As above.*]

" My handsome little son, never fall in love,
Who falls in love can never be saved!"

LEOPOLDO.

Eh! . . . Oliva! . . . do you hear that song?
Who can tell how it ever came up to these heights!
It's the song that all the mothers sing where I
come from! . . . They all say, Don't fall in
love! . . . And we sail all around the globe, escape
from the mouths of sharks . . . and on one fine
day look into two eyes, and if they look back, we're
done for . . . They must have sung the same song
to you, Oliva, when you were a little one . . .
Otherwise . . .

OLIVA.

I? Who told you so?

LEOPOLDO.

[Embracing her.]

Don't you think that when this little heart cries
out it can be heard even outside? . . . When you see
a nest, do you have to break it to find out whether
there's a brood inside? . . .

OLIVA.

[Girlishly.]

I never break them. . . . understand? I never,
never break nests! When I was a little girl, well . . .
I did, then, for I was bad . . . But it's a long time
since there's been any danger of that . . . Sometimes, do you know what I do? I climb up to a
nest, and every fledgling I find I kiss on its little
head . . . Then I leave it twittering and run
away! . . .

LEOPOLDO.

[*With a rapid gesture he encircles Oliva's head.*]
A kiss upon its little head! . . . Let *me* give *you*
one, too! . . [*He kisses her passionately upon the cheek.*]

> [*Bistone's heavy steps are heard. Leopoldo
> frees Oliva, who runs toward the room in
> which Riga is putting the children to sleep.*]

OLIVA.

[*With forced calm.*]

Mamma . . . Has he fallen asleep?

> [*While Leopoldo drops into a chair, his head
> resting upon his right palm and his elbow
> upon the table, Bistone comes in with the
> goat across his shoulder.*]

BISTONE.

[*Stopping as soon as he enters.*]

Oliva? . . . Riga? . . . What? They've left you
here all alone? . . . And I was going to wait for her.
Much thought these women give to the animals,
eh? If it weren't for me! No use talking! Here
she is [*laying the goat upon the pallet.*] She might
have died.

LEOPOLDO.

[*Gathering his wits, somewhat distractedly.*]
It's very ill, eh? . . .

BISTONE.

[As if recalling.]

I had you in mind, too, you may be sure. I told "Dente di legno" to pass this way, so that he can mount you on a donkey . . . In a couple of hours you'll reach the Quattro Strade.

LEOPOLDO.

But . . . with this heavy downpour . . .

BISTONE.

[Laughing.]

To'! What have you been doing all this time? Haven't you seen how starry the sky is? Just come and take a look. See how many there are . . . And it's not yet night.

LEOPOLDO.

By God! *[Arises and steps outside the door, followed by Bistone.]*

BISTONE.

If I were to present you with as many sheep as there are stars in the sky this minute, I'll wager my head that you'd become a shepherd, too.

LEOPOLDO.

How beautiful! And what a delicious cool breeze! . . . *[He remains gazing at the horizon about him while Bistone strides grumblingly to the door at the right.]*

BISTONE.

[Shouting.]

Oliva! By Diana!

RIGA.

[*From within, her voice stifled with rage.*]
Stop that bawling! . . . I had just fallen asleep,
too! Go, Oliva!

> [*In a moment Oliva appears, still utterly con-*
> *fused. As if shunning her father's glances*
> *she sits down beside the goat.*]

BISTONE.

> [*Takes the oil lamp from the table and carries*
> *it near to the pallet.*]

And I was going to wait for you, Oliva! Even you
no longer care for these poor little creatures. Just
look at it . . . it doesn't move . . . and the red
eyes it has! . . . And she's burning as if she were
baked! What do you think ails her? . . .

OLIVA.

> [*Murmuring.*]

Why! [*Continues to stroke the goat.*]

RIGA.

> [*Coming in.*]

Very well . . . Let's have a look . . . Let's see
. . . Is she dead yet? [*Ironically.*]

LEOPOLDO.

> [*Returns. — The yearning for some distant*
> *port has already transfigured his counte-*
> *nance. He approaches Oliva and she, for a*
> *moment, suspends her examination, without*
> *however raising her eyes.*]

So then? She's really very sick . . Poor little
creature! . . .

Bistone.

What do you say to that? Oliva ought to understand! The other time she gave la Rosa a certain
drink of her own brewing . . . No use talking . . .
The creature got well and was better than ever! But
today . . . She seems half in tears . . . What do I
know? . . . There must be something on her
mind! . . .

Riga.

Well, Oliva! We're waiting to hear what you have
to say. Why so silent?

Oliva.

She . . . she's sick, all right . . . But I . . .
I can't say what's the trouble with her.

Riga.

[Laughing.]

She must be in love, then!

> *[Dragging footsteps are heard. Leopoldo is the
> only one who turns to look at the newcomer.
> It is Gigi. The youth sees them all staring
> at the pallet, so he looks, too. Having learned
> what the matter is, he turns without a word
> toward the fireplace, where the wood is still
> burning, and sits down as comfortably as
> possible upon the stone.]*

BISTONE.

Examine her well, Oliva. It doesn't seem possible! This time it seems you don't care to cure her. Look into her ears. Try to make her drink something, and see how she swallows it . . . No use talking . . . Just look at her.

LEOPOLDO.

[*Takes a basin, fills it from a jug and hands it to Oliva.*]

Here, Oliva. See if it's her throat that's bothering her.

[*Oliva, in the greatest confusion, takes the basin and thrusts the goat's snout into it, while the three bend over to watch the result. Pause.*]

RIGA.

She swallows it real well! I told you so! She's in love! . . . That's all that ails her! Let her have a good sleep, and tomorrow she'll be romping about . . . Better go to milk, for the night's already an hour old . . . [*Goes to the fireplace, hurriedly gets the milk pails ready, while Bistone, sulking, empties the basin of water.*]

LEOPOLDO.

An hour? It must be eight! By God! How quickly the time flew! [*As if in meditation.*] And tomorrow evening . . . at this hour . . . on the sea again!

OLIVA.

[*With a piercing cry.*]
Oh the sea . . . Tomorrow evening! . . .

> [*Leopoldo looks distractedly at Riga and Bistone, so that Oliva may gaze at him to her heart's content. She fixes her desperate virginal eyes upon his hardy, handsome features. During this instant, amidst the stupidity of Gigi, the unconscious egoism of Leopoldo and the simplicity of her parents, a silent drama reaches its climax in Oliva's tender soul.*]

RIGA.

[*Going over to the sink and tugging at Bistone's jacket.*]

Leave everything to Oliva. You don't know a thing about it. Take these pails. Just see how they glisten! [*She puts two pails into his hands.*] Gigi! Are you asleep there, too? Mother of mine, save him! Take the pails!

BISTONE.

[*Placing the two pails on the floor.*]
Wait a bit. I want to warm my hands a little. I'm cold this evening. It must be the years piling up.

> [*Gigi, who had half risen, sinks comfortably down upon the stone again. Leopoldo, leaning against the door-jamb, turns to gaze upon Oliva, who lowers her head sadly.*]

LEOPOLDO.

Oliva . . . [*Somewhat louder.*] Oliva . . . Why don't you look at me any more? [*Fingering the little basket upon the table.*] Did you make this beautiful basket?

OLIVA.

[*Hurriedly raises her eyes. A brief rebirth of hope brings a fleeting smile.*]

Yes . . . I made it . . . But I couldn't finish it . . . You see, I lost my knife . . .

LEOPOLDO.

Poor Oliva! . . . Take this one. [*Unpocketing his Catalonian knife.*] See how beautiful it is! I bought it in America . . . Who could have guessed that I was buying it for you! . . . It'll be a souvenir of me. [*He opens it. The three springs cause Bistone and Riga to turn about at the same time.*]

BISTONE.

What are you doing there? . . . Do you want to cut her throat?

RIGA.

Heaven forbid! . . .

LEOPOLDO.

[*To the parents.*]

No, no . . . I won't touch your little goat. I was showing Oliva how these Catalonian knives are made.

RIGA.

Ah! . . .

LEOPOLDO.

[*To Oliva.*]

And this is how you close it. [*He closes it.*]

OLIVA.

[*Looks at the knife in infinite despair.*]

Couldn't you give me something else to remember you by? . . . Something less pretty . . . and less expensive? . . .

LEOPOLDO.

Don't say that, my dear Oliva. Why do you talk that way? . . . If you only knew what pleasure it gives me to think that this big knife of mine will be in your soft little hands! And that you'll be working away at your reeds, quietly, far up in these mountains, and thinking of me every time you use it! Winter's coming on. Ugly weather at sea. Many sailors lose their lives! [*The tinkling of a coalman's bell, like that in the early part of the act, becomes more and more distinct.*]

DENTE DI LEGNO.

[*Outside.*]

Whoa-a-a-! [*The bell stops tinkling.*] Ho, there, Bistone! Here we are! . . .

BISTONE.

[*At the sound of the bell he has risen from his seat before the hearth. He takes the four pails in his left hand.*]

Dente di legno! [*To the coalman, who enters.*]
Here's your gentleman. Have you remembered to
polish up your best saddle?

DENTE DI LEGNO.

You rascally devil! . . . Whom do you take me
for? . . . I've even put a new package on it, into
the bargain!

LEOPOLDO.

[*Goes to take his cap from under the fireplace.*]
Bravo! And can we reach the Quattro Strade by
ten?

DENTE DI LEGNO.

If we leave at once . . .

LEOPOLDO.

Then will you be securing this valise in the meantime?

DENTE DI LEGNO.

Right away. [*Takes the valise and is about to leave.*]

LEOPOLDO.

[*To the coalman.*]
We don't dismount during the journey, do we?
Do I have to wear these boots?

DENTE DI LEGNO.

No stops! You leave here and dismount at the
Quattro Strade. [*Exit.*]

LEOPOLDO.

[*To Bistone.*]

Then will you take these boots, eh, Bistone?

What? . . . Do you really mean it? . . . A pair of new boots? I don't want them . . . They may come in handy to you.

RIGA.

If Signor Leopoldo has no use for them . . .

LEOPOLDO.

Yes, yes . . . Take them . . . You'll please me very much by accepting them as a remembrance of me.

BISTONE.

Really? . . . Why this is too much . . .

RIGA.

So you're going back to your sailing, Signor Leopoldo? To your sailing over the sea? Lord knows how many years we'll keep remembering you . . . and you, on the other hand, in two or three days, will have forgotten all about us!

LEOPOLDO.

Why should I forget you? If we sailors shouldn't recall folks, how could we live? We'd die of monotony!

RIGA.

Oliva! [*Oliva is caressing the goat convulsively.*] Why don't you stand up and say good-bye to the gentleman! Or have you lost your head, too, with this little creature? Come and bid Signor Leopoldo farewell! [*Oliva still strokes the animal. Then she arises in confusion. Without raising her glance she approaches Riga.*]

LEOPOLDO.

Good-bye, Oliva . . . May heaven send you all that you desire, and make you happy!

RIGA.

Thank the gentleman! . . . What do you call this? . . . Have you caught the goat's illness?

OLIVA.

[*With infinite sadness.*]

Thank you!

BISTONE.

And don't ever come back to these parts, understand. They're not for you.

DENTE DI LEGNO.

[*Returning.*]

We're ready, master.

LEOPOLDO.

Good-bye, Bistone . . . Good luck to you, and thanks. Good-bye, Gigi.

RIGA.

[*To Gigi.*]

Listen, you beast! He's talking to you! Come here!

GIGI.

[*Takes two or three steps forward with the two pails in his hand. Murmurs.*]

Till we meet again. [*Oliva eyes him strangely.*]

RIGA.

"Till we meet again!" What are you talking about? Do you think that Signor Leopoldo's a coal-man like Pippo, who comes back when he's sold his load? Say "Good-bye" to him, can't you?

BISTONE.

Good luck, and long life to you!

RIGA.

Good health to you, and plenty of money! [*All leave through the back door except Oliva, who seems petrified. — Pause, while Leopoldo, who can no longer be seen, mounts his horse.*]

BISTONE.

[*In the doorway.*]

Are you comfortable on that saddle?

LEOPOLDO.

[*From outside.*]

Excellent!

DENTE DI LEGNO.

[*Outside.*]

We're off, then! [*Shouting loudly.*] Aiuuuu . . . Furia . . . [*The bell begins to tinkle; the horses start.*]

Riga.

Come, folks. Hurry. Get busy with the milking.

Bistone.

[To Riga.]

Put out the fire, won't you, Riga? And go to bed, for tomorrow we've got to get up an hour earlier. *[To Gigi.]* Get a move on. *[They leave. Gigi passes behind the window; Bistone stops behind the window, and turning toward the direction in which Leopoldo disappeared, he shouts "Good-by-y-y-y-y-ye!"]*

Leopoldo.

[From the distance.]

Good-by-y-y-y-y-ye!

Riga.

[Returns and hastens to the fireplace, speaking half to herself.]

Let's put out the fire, then. *[She empties the jug of water upon the brands, which, sputtering and smoking, are soon extinguished. At this moment Oliva leaves the doorway, from where she has been watching the departure of their guest. She throws herself down upon the pallet, beside the sick little goat, and bursts into a desperate weeping. Riga, in frightened amazement, turns around.]* What does this mean?

CURTAIN.

PERSONS

GASTONE, *An animal trainer.*

FIFI RAPETTA ⎱ *Sisters, and*
NENNE RAPETTA ⎰ *Marchionesses.*

BARONESS ANGELICA DEL BRANCO.

GASTONE
THE ANIMAL TAMER

Scene: *The room of the animal trainer, inside one of those huge circus wagons that make up the rear of the menageries. The stage is lighted only by two moonbeams that come in through the little open windows in the back wall. At each side wall, a closed door. To the left, along the back wall, a small, low bed, and nearby, a night-table upon which are placed a golden watch in its case and a tiny shaving mirror. Next to the bed, along the rear wall, a wash-stand, chairs, then a corner table with letters, papers, post-cards and an inkstand upon it. On the wall at the right, a medicine chest. All around the walls, whips, guns, pistols, photographs of women and of wild animals.*

At the rise of the curtain there comes, from nearby, the strident, raucously discordant music of brass instruments. Suddenly the music ceases in the very midst of a phrase. The profound silence that follows is broken by two or three feminine cries of terror, which are suddenly hushed. Then, a revolver shot, a furious crack of a whip, a clanking of chains, and at last, a vast round of frantic, fairly interminable applause, mingling with shouts from a deeply moved audience: "Bravo!" "Evviva!"

While the applause is dying out, the little door at the right is thrust open, and Gastone, the animal trainer, appears. He turns on the electric lights. He is sweating freely, his manner portraying the strain he has just gone through; his reddened face is almost the color of his flaming garb in the Russian manner, with its large black frogs. His long dark hair has fallen across his eyes, which roll flashingly in their sockets. He is still trembling with rage in every muscle. Strong, triumphant, he bursts into, rather than enters, the room and the boards of the floor creak beneath his glittering boots. Behind him, through the door that he has left open, and unseen by him, come Fifi and Nenne hand in hand, sisters of sixteen and fifteen respectively. They are dressed in white, all laces and ribbons; blushing furiously, eager, and quivering with laughter, they remain standing upon the threshold.

GASTONE.

　　　[*As he enters, grumbles, among other unintelligible words.*]

That damned Fifi! . . . She'll pay for it! Tonight she'll get a supper of fork prongs instead of meat! [*He throws the revolver and the whip upon his bed, and, in the mirror upon the night-table, he looks at the scratches on his shoulder.*]

FIFI.

　　　　　　　　　　　　　　　[*To Nenne.*]

How handsome he is!

NENNE.

　　　　　　　　　　　　　　　[*To Fifi.*]

How handsome he is!

GASTONE.

[*Touching one of the scratches, and grumbling, as above.*]

I had that plagued beast so well trained to jump on me without mussing me up so! . . . Bah! [*He turns around. Beholding the young strangers he stares at them in wonderment.*]

FIFI AND NENNE.

[*Embrace each other tightly. The first moves as if to escape.*]

GASTONE.

[*With the politeness of an athlete.*]

My dear young ladies! You needn't run away! Why? I don't eat little girls!

FIFI.

[*Turns back, still clasping Nenne's hand.*]

GASTONE.

And what did these noble young ladies desire of the animal-trainer Gastone?

FIFI AND NENNE.

[*Look at each other and laugh.*]

GASTONE.

But won't you come in?

FIFI.

[*To Nenne, looking about.*]

How charming everything is in here!

GASTONE.

[*To Fifi.*]

Really? . . . But perhaps. . . . For the first five minutes, everything is charming!

FIFI.

Even we! Who have come to bore you! [*Nenne laughs.*]

GASTONE.

Ah, but you would be charming . . . for all eternity!

FIFI.

Don't exaggerate!

GASTONE.

Please make yourselves comfortable. . . .[*Offering chairs.*] Is there any one with you?

FIFI AND NENNE.

No, no! We are alone!

GASTONE.

Ah!

FIFI.

There isn't the slightest thing wrong about this.

GASTONE.

Quite the contrary!

FIFI AND NENNE.

For we've come to. . . .

GASTONE.

[*Laughing.*]

To . . . ? The rest is easy to guess: To look at close range upon a man who was on the point of being devoured. Isn't that so? [*Fifi and Nenne clasp each other in admiration of his prowess.*] But, my dear young ladies, it's no easy matter to devour Gastone the animal-trainer! . . . My hair's a bit rumpled, and there are a few rips in my jacket. But here I am, no parts missing, as you can see!

FIFI.

Heavens, what an eternal minute that was!

NENNE.

What a horrible minute!

FIFI.

You were simply magnificent! I was the first one to shout "Bravo!" too.

NENNE.

No. *I* was really the first.

FIFI.

That's not at all so!

NENNE.

You're a story-teller!

GASTONE.

Peace, peace, peace! You were both the first. There! I saw you perfectly.

FIFI AND NENNE.

Uh! Really? You saw us?

GASTONE.

Yes . . . yes, indeed. . . . And I also caught sight of a crowd of women nearby. . . .

FIFI AND NENNE.

Ah! That was our stupid mamma. . . . She fainted. . . . She's always fainting. . . . They must have taken her out. . . .

GASTONE.

Oh! This is not at all to my liking!

FIFI.

Why?

GASTONE.

Eh?

FIFI

If mother hadn't swooned, how could we ever have come to you here?

GASTONE.

[*To Fifi.*]

Ah! Looking at the matter in that light! . . .

FIFI.

Do you know, we have a terrible mother? We have!

NENNE.

Awful!

GASTONE.

An animal-trainer of the old school, I suppose!

NENNE.

You laugh! Because you don't know what it means to be continually spied upon by two eyes as big as this [*Distends her eyes*].

FIFI.

. . . That see everything!

NENNE.

For twenty-four hours a day!

GASTONE.

And . . . suppose your mother were right?

FIFI AND NENNE.

No, no! She's wrong! Damned wrong! For it's all useless!

FIFI.

. . . Because we're not made like all the other young ladies!

GASTONE.

Oh! Hear, hear!

FIFI.

We weren't born to do what all the rest do!

GASTONE.

Eh!

NENNE.

Indeed! For we. . . .

FIFI.

We're of the kind that are destined to great things. That's why! . . .

NENNE.

One of those careers that gets your name in the papers! . . .

GASTONE.

Eh!

FIFI. '

. . . and then in the novels!

NENNE.

It's no use. These are things that are felt inside.

FIFI.

And you can understand us!

NENNE.

Yes! *You* can!

GASTONE.

I?

FIFI.

Yes, for you're not like all those imbeciles of the summer colony. [*Gastone bows.*]

NENNE.

What a strange life yours must be!

FIFI.

What a wonderful novel your life must make!

NENNE.

Who can tell what adventures led to your becoming an animal-tamer!

FIFI.

If we could only find out!

GASTONE.

Animal-tamer? Why, I can tell you right away! Because my father, heaven rest his soul, was an animal-trainer, and I. . . .

FIFI AND NENNE.

Oh dear! Really? Oh! What a sin! [*Disillusioned.*]

GASTONE.

What a sin? . . . Why?

FIFI.

But . . . simply that? . . .

NENNE.

If you only knew what stories we've read . . . about tamers! . . .

FIFI.

Marvellous tales! . . .

NENNE.

Just imagine. There was one who was nothing less than an American millionaire. . . .

GASTONE.

Lucky dog!

FIFI.

. . . and through love . . .

NENNE.

. . . through love of a French princess . . .

FIFI AND NENNE.

. . . he became an animal trainer!

GASTONE.

Oh! There's a strange fellow for you! I'd prefer the contrary!

FIFI AND NENNE.

What do you mean?

GASTONE.

Through love of a princess . . . I'd like to become a millionaire!

FIFI AND NENNE.

[*Disgusted.*]

Oh! What horrid things you say!

GASTONE.

Horrid?

FIFI.

[*To Nenne.*]

But do you believe him? Do you think he's speaking seriously? How silly we've been!

GASTONE.

Why?

FIFI.

[*To Gastone.*]

No, no, it's all our fault! You are perfectly right! One doesn't tell one's most intimate secrets to the first person who happens to come along!

GASTONE.

Why, nothing of the sort!

NENNE.

[*Pouting.*]

We . . . are . . . the first to come along! . . .

FIFI.

True enough! And we should have understood it!

GASTONE.

But I assure you . . . that you're mistaken!
How can I help it if I'm not an amateur, a dilettante,
but a born animal-tamer, who grew up among wild
beasts, have lived among wild beasts all my life and
will die among wild beasts. . . .

NENNE.

. . and decolleté women!

FIFI.

Nenne!

NENNE.

Can't you see that the walls here are covered with
pictures of wild beasts and bare-necked women?

FIFI.

Very well. But you oughtn't to say such things,
because you're a baby. . . .

GASTONE.

Ha, ha, ha! [*To Fifi, laughing.*] This woman's
air really becomes you!

FIFI.

[*Interrupts him, in a rage.*]

"This woman's air!" Then you imagine I'm not a woman!

GASTONE.

But! . . . [*Laughing.*] So so!

FIFI.

[*More furious than ever.*]

Aha! "So so"? It's very evident that you understand only beasts and . . . women of that sort there! . . . [*She turns her back childishly upon him and stands near the table.*]

[*A note enclosed in an envelope comes flying in through one of the open windows and falls at Nenne's feet.*]

NENNE.

Uh! [*Jumps back in fear.*]

GASTONE.

[*Very quickly dashes to pick it up, agitated.*]

Ah! You'll pardon me, won't you? This is, er, a very important message. . . .

FIFI.

You can tell that from the way it came in!

NENNE.

. . . and you can scent it from the perfume it exhales.

GASTONE.

[*Mumbling the letter in an unintelligible manner, and then, aloud.*]

. . . At half-past-eleven sharp.

FIFI.

[*With lightning-like rapidity she seizes the gold watch before her on the table and turns the hands back.*

That's done! Now I've fixed him. [*Having done this, she begins to look herself over in the mirror.*]

GASTONE.

[*Continues to mutter other unintelligible words, then folds the letter and puts it into his jacket pocket.*]

You will excuse me, won't you? You've heard. . . . It's an appointment for half-past-eleven sharp. . . . A very urgent matter. . . . [*Turning toward the table.*] And I must dress. . . . And there's only ten minutes to spare. . . . [*Takes up his watch, looks at it, and makes a gesture of great surprise.*] Eh! [*He puts the watch to his ear.*] But it's going!

FIFI.

[*With studied indifference.*]

What's the trouble?

GASTONE.

When I came in it was ten minutes to eleven.

FIFI.

[*As above.*]

And what time is it now?

GASTONE.

Eleven. . . . Can it be possible? It's surely no less than half an hour since. . . .

FIFI.

Thanks, ever so much!

GASTONE.

What do you mean?

FIFI.

It's really not very polite to give young ladies to understand that a ten-minute visit seemed all of half an hour!

NENNE.

I should say so. [*Gastone looks from one to the other.*]

FIFI.

But if your affairs are so urgent, we'll leave just the same.

GASTONE.

You must understand. . . . Really, it's a matter of . . . meat . . . for my animals. . . . It's a very good bargain . . . I might miss it!

FIFI AND NENNE.

Ah! Meat? . . . For your animals?

FIFI.

Very well. Very well. We'll leave. [*Spreading her veil across her shoulders.*] We'll leave at once! [*Showing little desire, however, to go.*]

GASTONE.

[*Offering his hand.*]

My most noble young ladies!

FIFI.

Oh! Your hand? Not at all! You don't deserve it! I don't forgive so soon! [*She turns to the right.*]

GASTONE.

So cruel?

FIFI.

[*Turning suddenly around.*]

Don't you like it?

GASTONE.

Of course I don't like it! Come now, like good girls, tell me what I can do to win your pardon.

NENNE.

As far as I'm concerned, let me have one of those beautiful post-cards with your picture and a flourishing autograph, and I'll be satisfied!

GASTONE.

[*Going to the table.*]

That's quickly done! Here! [*Nenne claps her hands and dances about, but Fifi remains serious.*]

NENNE.

Uh! What a beautiful signature!

GASTONE.

And we'll put down the inscription, too. To Miss Nenne. . . isn't that right?

NENNE.

Marchioness Nenne Rapetta.

GASTONE.

[*Writing.*]

Very happy! . . . And do you come from hereabouts?

NENNE.

Yes. But we spend the winter in Florence.

GASTONE.

[*Having signed a second card.*]

And this is for your elder sister. . . . What is her name?

FIFI.

The same as your tiger's. . . . [*disdainfully.*]

GASTONE.

Fifi? . . . Oh! I'm so glad to hear that!

FIFI.

Yes, Fifi! And look at the fine claws I have, too! [*She thrusts her ten finger-nails in a row directly under his nose.*]

GASTONE.

Perbacco!

FIFI.

And let me tell you that I'm not satisfied with that gift there! . . .

GASTONE.

No?

FIFI.

No. I want a different one. . . . It's something you're going to throw away in any event! . . . So. . . .

GASTONE.

Indeed! Tell me what. . . .

FIFI.

Oh, nothing. Simply the note you just got from the butcher. . . . [*Looking at his coat pocket, whence protrudes the letter referred to.*]

GASTONE.

[*Not understanding.*]

The note from the butch . . . ?

FIFI.

[*Who in the meantime, with feline agility, has snatched the letter out of his pocket and flourishes it in her hand.*]

Here it is! The gift is already made! [*Nenne bursts with laughter.*]

GASTONE.

Ah! This is too much! [*Rises, ill able to control his consternation.*] I hope this is only a joke. [*Goes to the door at the right and closes it.*]

FIFI.

[*Evading him.*]

But isn't this a letter from the butcher? What can you do with it?

GASTONE.

Ah! No, no! Be a good girl, now! Give me that letter! . . . Marchioness Nenne, help me recover that note!

FIFI.

But just see how fond he is of that butcher! [*Dodging him, laughingly.*]

GASTONE.

That letter belongs to me. I beg you! I warn you, now, that if you don't return it I'll be compelled to take it by force!

FIFI.

Really! Oh! How excellent! [*With a mingling of girlish and feline glee she prepares to defend her prey.*]

NENNE.

Fie, Fifi! Give it . . . back! [*There is a short struggle between Gastone and Fifi.*]

GASTONE.

That letter, I say! [*He pursues her.*]

FIFI.

[*Flourishing the note.*]

Here it is!

GASTONE.

You just wait! [*Threateningly.*]

FIFI.

Yes! You think it's easy, don't you! [*She evades him.*]

GASTONE.

It won't be impossible, though! . . .

FIFI.

You'll find me worse than that other Fifi!

NENNE.

Fie! It's a shame, Fifi!

GASTONE.

This little arm is mine! It won't escape again!

FIFI

[*Passing the letter to her other hand.*]

But the letter escapes!

NENNE.

Dear me! Fifi!

GASTONE.

[*Still struggling with her.*]

And now we'll capture this other little arm!

FIFI.

[*Trying to free herself.*]

No! no! I say!

GASTONE.

Here it is, caught! . . . Ow! Ouch! !

FIFI.

Have I hurt you?

GASTONE.

[*Taking advantage of the moment to snatch the letter from her hand.*

Oh! At last! [*Triumphantly he conceals the recaptured letter in his inside pocket.*]

FIFI.

[*Filled with scorn.*]

Ah! Wicked fellow!

NENNE.

[*At first uncertain, and then with confidence, takes Gastone's right hand.*]

But goodness me! She really *has* hurt you! Look!

GASTONE.

It's nothing!

NENNE.

Your wrist . . . is all scratched up! Why, Fifi!

FIFI.

Is it possible? [*Runs to see.*]

GASTONE.

Why, it's a mere trifle!

FIFI.

[*Genuinely affected.*]

Oh, dear me! What a long scratch! However could I have done it! It's always that way. I never realize it. . . .

NENNE.

But the persons who get the scratch realize it.

GASTONE.

No, no, I say. Let there be peace. It will be a souvenir that will disappear only too soon! . . . [*Glancing at the watch, and, with evident desire to be rid of them, extending his hand.*] A nice handshake, now!

NENNE.

But are you going to leave that wound as it is?

GASTONE.

Wound? [*Laughing.*]

FIFI.

It certainly needs attention!

GASTONE.

Attention? . . . What the deuce are you talking about! I'll cure it with a little fresh water! [*Again he extends his hand and walks toward the door with them, as if to accompany them out.*] You may run along, then, and rest easy on that score. . . .

FIFI.

[*In confusion.*]

No, no, no! Not at all easy!

NENNE.

Take care! Finger-nail scratches are dangerous! We know all about it, we do! Our mamma is a Lady of the Red Cross! We'll make you a model bandage! You'll see!

GASTONE.

By no means!

FIFI.

Yes, I say! You'll see how content you'll be after it's done. After the accident that happened to you this evening I thought of a beautiful bandage on your arm!

NENNE.

It will be twice as interesting! You'll see what an effect it will have upon the ladies! [*Runs to the medicine chest.*]

FIFI.

And also upon your . . . butcher!

GASTONE.

Upon my butch . . . ! [*Understanding her insinuation, he is somewhat provoked.*] Ah! I beg you leave me. Don't insist. [*Showing his wrist.*] Can't you see, it's all better!

NENNE.

[*Returning with plenty of cotton, gauze, iodine and other ingredients.*]

Here's all we need!

FIFI.

Good for you, Nenne! Place the stuff there! [*Points to a chair.*]

GASTONE.

Oh! Here's a pretty mess! Where did you get all that hospital?

NENNE.

Inside there! Don't you think I know a medicine chest when I see one? At a glance!

FIFI.

Get me a basin.

GASTONE.

But I don't want this! I can attend to my own needs, at my convenience.

FIFI.

You keep still! You can't imagine how extraordinarily striking you'll look with your arm in a sling. . . . Everybody asking you: "What's this? What's this?" and you, curling your mustache: "Oh, nothing, nothing. A present from that rascally Fifi!" . . . And you won't be telling a lie! . . . [*She laughs, and for a moment Gastone himself cannot help laughing.*] What wouldn't I give to be there when you say that! . . .

NENNE.

[*Laughing as she prepares the various articles for the operation, arraying them upon three chairs ranged in a row.*]

Ah! How beautiful!

GASTONE.

[*Looking impatiently at his watch, raises his eyes desparingly to the ceiling. Aside.*]

If good Saint Anthony would only do me the favor of sending their mother after them!

FIFI.

What's that?

GASTONE.

After all, you ought to remember that your mother must be anxious. . . .

NENNE.

That will make a fine opportunity to talk French!

GASTONE.

? !

FIFI AND NENNE.

Surely! When mamma is greatly excited she always talks French! . . . [*They laugh.*] She was educated at Geneva.

GASTONE.

Yes, yes. But if I were in your shoes, I'd give a serious — a really serious — thought to my affairs. [*Looks again at his watch, then puts it up to his ear.*]

FIFI AND NENNE.

[*Still busy with their medical preparations.*] Why?

GASTONE.

It doesn't seem to occur to you that some one may have seen you come this way.

FIFI AND NENNE.

Impossible! Utterly impossible!

GASTONE.

That's what *you* say!

FIFI.

Never you mind. There's no use in your trying to scare us. I refuse to surrender the pleasure of sending you about with this marvellous bandage that I'm making for you. Stop looking at that watch! Come here! You'll see what a wonderful bandage we have for you inside of five minutes!

NENNE.

Right away. Well, we're waiting for you.

FIFI.

Give your arm here.

GASTONE.

[*Resigned.*]

Very well. Here you are.

FIFI.

[*Rolling up his sleeves to the elbow and holding his arm over the basin.*]

The sublimate.

NENNE.

[*On the point of getting it, when she stops in admiration.*]

How beautiful! It looks exactly like that arm the monks had us copy this year. Isn't that so, Fifi?

FIFI.

[*Following with her thumb the outlines of the muscles and examining the arm from all sides.*]

In every detail!

GASTONE.

Ah! This is really charming!

FIFI.

Never you mind. You may well be proud. It was a copy of the statue of David!

GASTONE.

Ah! The famous David of Raphael!

FIFI AND NENNE.

No! Of Michelangelo!!

GASTONE.

Right you are! I'm always confusing those fellows. They were both of them such fine chaps! . . . But what are you doing? I don't want any of that vile smelling stuff!

FIFI AND NENNE.

Iodoform! You've got to! The devil! Leave these matters to persons who know! If it doesn't smell a little nobody'll believe it's a dangerous wound!

GASTONE.

That doesn't make a particle of difference to me!

FIFI.

You're wrong.

NENNE.

Just a little, little bit. There! So! [*Gastone looks helplessly at the ceiling and then at his watch.*]

FIFI.

Now the cotton. [*Nenne fetches a great quantity of cotton.*]

GASTONE.

Eh? Why you've got a mattress there!

FIFI.

It's necessary! You'll see what a bandage that'll be!

NENNE.

[*Winds a long roll of gauze around his arm.*]
Just take a look at that!

FIFI.

That isn't good at all! [*Takes the roll of gauze.*] Here! This is the way.

GASTONE.

My hand, too?

FIFI.

Of course! It'll look better.

NENNE.

It'll be more interesting.

FIFI.

You'll see what a demonstration you'll receive tomorrow evening!

NENNE.

[*Snatching the roll of gauze.*]
No not like that! I tell you that's not the way!

FIFI.

And I say it is!

NENNE.

It isn't!

FIFI.

It is!

NENNE.

It isn't! [*Alternately they snatch the roll of gauze out of each other's grasp.*]

GASTONE.

[*Listening.*]

Hush!

FIFI AND NENNE.

Eh? What is it? Good Lord! [*The roll falls to the ground.*]

GASTONE.

Sh! [*In a low voice.*] The dog's growling. Some stranger is approaching. . . .

FIFI AND NENNE.

[*Clasping each other.*]

Oh, Lord!

GASTONE.

Your mother, perhaps. . . . The footsteps are coming from this direction [*He indicates the left*] so that I'd advise you to escape at once that way. [*Points to the door at the right.*]

FIFI.

Escape? Impossible, signor Trainer! Our legs wouldn't stir. . . . Hide us!

NENNE.

Yes, yes!

GASTONE.

This is maddening!

[*Suddenly Fifi runs to the switch and turns off
the electric light.*]

NENNE.

What are you doing?

GASTONE.

What are you up to, confound it all!

NENNE.

You're making matters worse, I tell you.

FIFI.

No! If they see it's dark, they won't know.
Because they'll be sure that we're not here.

NENNE.

But suppose they saw the light before. . . .

FIFI.

Then this gentleman will certainly find a way to
hide us. . . .

GASTONE.

So! You think so, do you? Well, instead, I'll
throw the door wide open to your mother! And
I'll shout my innocence, and be well believed!
You'll see. . . .

A Woman's Voice.

Gastone! [*After an instant of surprise, the sides, psychologically speaking, are reversed. Gastone is astounded, while the two young ladies are seized with a mad desire to dance.*]

Fifi.

[*To Gastone.*]

You have a caller! [*Laughs.*]

Gastone.

[*Rolling his eyes, threatening with his finger, and speaking with a stifled voice.*]

That watch was tampered with! It's half-past eleven!

Fifi.

[*Quickly.*]

Then it's the butcher! [*Nenne bursts into laughter.*]

Gastone.

[*With wild gestures demanding silence.*]

Sh!

The Voice.

[*Somewhat louder.*]

Gastone!

Fifi and Nenne.

And now? Where are you going to put us?

Gastone.

[*Beyond himself.*]

I'm going to send you off! All the worse for you.
. . . It's your fault if you're found here. I did my

best to get you out in time. . . . Now I'm going out to see this lady. In the meantime, make your escape by gliding along the side of the wagon. The dog is held in a short leash, so there's no fear on that score.

THE VOICE.

[*Louder and impatient.*]

Gastone!

GASTONE.

[*Trying to impart sweet accents to a voice quivering with excitement.*]

Oh! I am here. . . dear. . . .

THE VOICE.

Were you asleep? And this dog? . . .

GASTONE.

He's tied. Come nearer. . . .

THE VOICE.

[*Drawing near.*]

Ah! Beneath your window . . . by the light of the moon. . . . Do you want me to sing you a serenade? . . .

GASTONE.

You look so beautiful, all black in the white shimmer of the moon! [*He makes signs to the two girls to escape.*]

THE VOICE.

Have you become a poet?

GASTONE.

[*At his wits' end.*]

Indeed! [*Makes new signs, as above, but in vain. Fifi and Nenne clasp each other by the hand and communicate their impressions by means of repeated pressures and stifled shrieks.*]

FIFI.

Is it she?

NENNE.

Can't you hear? It's she!

FIFI.

[*Scornfully.*]

Always she.

NENNE.

Disgusting.

FIFI.

She, all the time.

THE VOICE.

But what are you doing with your hand behind there?

GASTONE.

[*Taking advantage of the moment to glare at Fifi and Nenne.*]

Nothing, nothing. I was bandaging a hand. . . . [*Cuts the gauze, holds his head stiff, then makes a vain effort to pull back his coat sleeve.*]

THE VOICE.

Did you hurt yourself? I must see.

GASTONE.

No, no! Stay there yet a moment. You are so beautiful! [*Renews his desperate signalling to Fifi and Nenne.*]

FIFI.

"So beautiful!" Yes, we know her! So well done up, he means!

NENNE.

She weighs as much as both of us put together. What can a man do with all that tonnage?

FIFI.

You think she's really a baroness!

NENNE.

She was a nursemaid!

FIFI.

She married her employer.

NENNE.

And then she made him die of a broken heart!

FIFI.

That's the kind of woman you love!

NENNE.

And if you ever heard the stories they tell of her!

FIFI.

She makes a specialty of aviators! [*Gastone, during this episode, has been making the most desperate gestures.*]

FIFI AND NENNE.

Yes, yes. We're going. Our best regards. Our compliments! [*They leave.*]

[*Gastone cannot restrain a deep sigh of relief.*]

THE VOICE.

What's the matter?

GASTONE.

I gaze upon you . . . and I sigh!

THE VOICE.

But have you really become a poet?

GASTONE.

My treasure! My fairest! Do you know, that was really a queer idea of yours. . . .

THE VOICE.

To wish to come here?

GASTONE.

Yes, in this circus wagon. I'm a bit upset. . . . I swear to you. . . . I couldn't believe that letter!

THE VOICE.

Silly boy! Open the door!

GASTONE.

[*Running to the door at the right.*]

It's open. Come in. [*He presses her hands in his.*] Angelica! [*He leads her in.*]

ANGELICA.

What mystery! [*Looking about the moonlit room.*] How happy I am that I came here! I never had such a rare experience!

GASTONE.

[*Offended.*]

So that I owe my good fortune to the whim of a baroness who wishes to experience. . . .

ANGELICA.

No, no! You big baby! [*Gives him a playful slap.*]

GASTONE.

If I were one of those men who lives in a brick house. . . .

ANGELICA.

No, no, no! There! You would be just as handsome. . . . [*About to kiss him.*]

GASTONE.

You mean it? [*Ready to kiss her.*]

[*Through the doorway may be caught a glimpse of Fifi, who, at the propitious moment, quickly reaches in and turns on the electric light. The kiss comes to nothing.*]

ANGELICA.

[*With a little cry, turns around.*]

GASTONE.

[*His eyes wide open, so as to discover the reason.*]

The light went on of its own accord.

ANGELICA.

No, no! I heard the switch turn very plainly.

GASTONE.

[*Goes to the door and investigates.*]

It must have been some mischievous urchin. . .

ANGELICA.

Close the door.

GASTONE.

[*As he closes the door.*]

They're regular devils!

ANGELICA.

It was so sweet and romantic in that mysterious light!

GASTONE.

That's easily managed! [*Turns off the light and then comes to her with open arms.*]

ANGELICA.

They gave me such a fright. . . . [*She sits down upon the cot.*]

GASTONE.

Fright? [*Caressing her, he takes out her hatpin, removes her hat, and sits down beside her, placing his arm about her waist.*]

ANGELICA.

Terrible!

GASTONE.

With Gastone the tamer at your side?

ANGELICA.

[*Holding his arm.*]

What a clumsy bandage! I didn't notice it before!
. . . And what an odor of chemicals! You've hurt
yourself very badly. . . .

GASTONE.

[*Uncertainly.*]

Oh! Nothing much. . . . A mere trifle. . . .

ANGELICA.

But how did it happen? . . . It couldn't have
been a wild beast . . . for instance?

GASTONE.

Er . . . that's it exactly,— a wild beast! . . .

ANGELICA.

A wild beast! . . . A tiger? Fifi? That terrible
Fifi? And to think I wasn't there? Ah! Why
didn't I come to this evening's performance?
[*Stroking his shoulders.*] And these are sc atches. . . .
She inflicted them! . . . Ah! . . .Tell me. . . .
What a fine sight it must have been! What a won-
derful success you must have scored! Tell me. . . .
Tell me all about it. . .

GASTONE.

Er . . . well. . . . She sprang for my neck. . .
with the most wicked intentions!

ANGELICA.

And then? [*Eagerly.*]

GASTONE.

And then, I side-stepped her and struck with the whip across the eyes. . .

ANGELICA.

Dear me! And then? [*With growing excitement.*]

GASTONE.

I left the cage!

ANGELICA.

[*Disappointed.*]

Is that all?

GASTONE.

What else was I to do?

ANGELICA.

How clumsy you fellows are at telling a story!

GASTONE.

Who?

ANGELICA.

Yes! You're all alike! The same as the aviators. You'd imagine they were telling you what they had for breakfast!

GASTONE.

Ah! That's so, is it?

ANGELICA.

Yes, it is so! And the ones who do tell a story well . . . are the fellows who've never made a flight.

GASTONE.

Do you know many of them? . . . They say. . . .

ANGELICA.

Oh, dear! Are you jealous? Don't worry, for in this moment, battered and torn as you are, conqueror of Fifi, I wouldn't swap you for the entire French aerial fleet! [*She throws her arms around his neck.*]

[*A handful of pebbles comes rattling in through the window and falls with a loud racket into the basin. This kiss, too, fails.*]

ANGELICA.

[*Shrieks again.*]

GASTONE.

[*Gets up, furious.*]

By the living God! This is too much!

ANGELICA.

I can't understand it!

GASTONE.

[*Going to the door.*]

Those confounded ragamuffins! They're as treacherous as cats!

ANGELICA.

But those ragamuffins of yours are experts at choosing the right moment!

GASTONE.

Just let me step out for a second with my whip! Wait! [*Turns on the light and leaves by the right door, whip in hand.*]

[*The snapping of the whip is heard together with the trainer's heavy footsteps upon the sand path. Angelica peers through the window when all of a sudden Fifi and Nenne come running in through the door at the right.*]

FIFI AND NENNE.

[*In confusion.*]

Baroness! Baroness del Branco! We saw you come in! We've come to ask you for help!

ANGELICA.

[*Turning around, at first frightened and then overwhelmed with confusion.*]

Eh? Ah! Help?

FIFI AND NENNE.

Yes, help. You can save us! You *must* save us!

ANGELICA.

But. . . . Yes, but how. . . .

FIFI.

Mother's looking for us . . . over land and sea. . . .

NENNE.

We took a long walk all by ourselves along the beach.

FIFI.

You know we're a tiny bit wild.

ANGELICA.

Oh! . . . You're such darling little things!

FIFI.

Yes, but mother doesn't think so. And we're afraid to go back home alone!

NENNE.

You accompany us back! Be a good dear!

ANGELICA.

[*Composing herself with an effort.*]

Oh! If it's only that. . . .

FIFI.

You'll tell her that we were all out walking together. . . .

NENNE.

And then mother'll have nothing to scold us for! Be a good dear!

ANGELICA.

[*Anything but delighted.*]

Certainly! With pleasure! . . . Especially as my duty here is accomplished. . . .

FIFI.

Excuse me for asking, but. . . . What duty?

ANGELICA.

[*Now complete mistress of herself, with the most tender air, pointing to the seats upon*

*which the articles from the medicine chest
have been left standing.*]

Can't you see? Nurse duty!

FIFI AND NENNE.

Oh!

ANGELICA.

Didn't you hear the news?

FIFI.

No!

ANGELICA.

Then you weren't to the circus this evening?

FIFI.

No!

NENNE.

No!

ANGELICA.

The animal-tamer Gastone had a very narrow
escape!

FIFI AND NENNE.

Really?

ANGELICA.

That terrible Fifi leaped at his neck to tear him
to pieces. A cold wave of terror passed over the
multitude. I had to shut my eyes. Suddenly we
beheld him, bleeding but smiling. . . .

FIFI AND NENNE.

[*Unable to restrain their laughter.*]

Oh, dear! Really?

ANGELICA.

And safe, yes, safe! Oh, what a moment was that! [*Growing excited.*] I'll never forget it if I live to be a hundred! They carried him here in triumph! He was a real hero! Oh!

FIFI.

And the wound?

ANGELICA.

His wrist. The blood spurted. . . . Ugh! How that blood spurted . . . yet he absolutely refused to have it treated. . . . At last, however, we persuaded him. . . .

GASTONE.

[*Outside, snapping his whip and grumbling.*]

Where could those wretches have hidden. . . . [*Enters and stands as if transfixed.*] What!

FIFI.

This gentleman, if I am not mistaken, is the animal-trainer Gastone!

NENNE.

Yes, yes!

ANGELICA.

Indeed it is. The triumphant tamer who gave a lesson to his rebellious beast. I believe. . . .

FIFI.

Permit me to clasp your hand!

NENNE.

Me, too! [*Angelica puts on her hat before the mirror.*]

FIFI.

We have just learned from the Baroness del Branco what a narrow escape you had, and of the wound you sustained in your arm. . . . Allow us to offer you our heartiest congratulations!

NENNE.

Our sincerest felicitations!

FIFI.

No one could have treated you better than the Baroness!

ANGELICA.

Oh! I am happy to have done what little I could. . . .

FIFI.

[*Insinuatingly.*]

You would have liked to do far more!

GASTONE.

[*Amazed.*]

What, what? Are you leaving? . . .

FIFI.

We must be getting home directly. And the Baroness, in her usual gracious manner, is accompanying us.

GASTONE.

Ah! . . .

FIFI.

[*Standing aside.*]

Lead the way, Baroness!

NENNE.

[*At the other side of the Baroness.*]

Lead the way!

[*Angelica, as she leaves, bows to Gastone, who looks daggers at her.*]

FIFI.

[*To Nenne.*]

You first.

NENNE.

[*To Gastone.*]

Till we meet again!

FIFI.

Till we meet again!

[*Gastone, bursting with rage, allows them to leave without returning their greetings. As the women's voices die away, he strides in from the threshold. Red in the face, his fists tightly clenched, he begins to pace to and fro in his room, with long steps, like a caged lion.*]

FIFI.

[*Reappearing.*]

Will you ever tell me again that I'm not a woman? [*With the roar of a wild beast Gastone dashes to the door. — Fifi escapes.*]

CURTAIN.

SABATINO LOPEZ

(1867–   )

Sabatino Lopez belongs to the intellectual group of modern Italian dramatists; born at Leghorn in the same year as Pirandello he is, like the noted Sicilian, a scholarly spirit who has been engaged as teacher, critic and writer of lively fiction; for a time he succeeded the widely known dramatist Marco Praga as president of the Authors' Society of Milan and for ten years served as dramatic critic upon the Genoese monthly, *Il Secolo XIX.*

Unlike so many of his confrères he is of a distinctly cosmopolitan outlook in his numerous plays; his work has been likened, for its various qualities, to the dramas of Dumas, of Hervieu, and of his countrymen Butti and Giacosa, yet comparison with the last-named playwright (which has gained currency through the few inadequate lines accorded Lopez in Tonelli's "L'Evoluzione del teatro contemporaneo in Italia") tends to obscure Lopez's personal traits. A fuller and more accurate view is that presented by Guido Ruberti in his "Il teatro contemporaneo in Europa" — a voluminous work which is more trustworthy for its long chapters upon the French and the Italian drama of recent days than for its uneven considerations of the play in other nations of Europe.

Lopez "represents among us," writes Ruberti, "that theatre which no longer is serious and which is not yet comic. . . . The most conspicuous characteristic of his work is, indeed, that frank wit of the Tuscan spirit which in every age has given to art its most exquisite and bizarre minds — that indefinable humor which was upon the lips of the Florentine rogue and the Pisan mercer, as sharp as a rapier-thrust and as pungent as truth." Like so much modern laughter in all the tongues, that of Lopez has a source of tears; he is not intent upon moralizing, preaching or philosophizing, although his conception of life recognizes the "dramatic contrast between the frailty of the flesh — a prey to passion that knows neither check nor law — and the supreme effort of the spirit, conscious of its lofty moral duties." Particularly applicable to the play by which he is here represented is the latter citation; Maria's punishment does not arise so much from any arbitrary imposition of a social prejudice as from her own momentary violation of a moral law in which she herself implicitly believes.

At bottom Lopez is a skeptic and an ironist; though he began as an avowed follower of the bitter truth — the theory of impassability connected with the "théâtre cruel" of which he was early a disciple — he became in the course of his writing a lover of the paradox which reveals that truth. His courtesans are often women fundamentally superior to their more "moral" sisters (*Ninetta*); true love is often forced to forego wedlock (*Il terzo marito*);

unselfish devotion is victimized by its own goodness (*La nostra pelle*); masculine ugliness finds it possible, by making a virtue of necessity and boldly creating an advantage out of a defect, to win more attention from the women than do the handsome fops (*Il brutto e le belle*). The play just named, it is interesting to note, has recently been adapted for performance in English, with Leo Dietrichstein in the role of the ugly banker who has in him a touch of the Cyrano.

There is much, then, of the Gallic in Lopez; in *La morale che corre* Ruberti discovers "the Italian type of the *comédie rosse*, of the audacious paradoxes dear to Ancey and to Wolff, filtered through an Italian mind that is all light and sentiment." If Lopez is not a dramatist of the first order he is easily one of the secondary personages who must be studied for a complete knowledge of the Italian theatre of today.

PERSONS

Maria Lòdoli	Cecchino
Signora Albini	Lisa
Lieutenant Graziani	Anna

A Little Boy of Two Years

THE SPARROW

Scene: *A room on the ground floor of a villetta in Varesotto. It is four o'clock of an afternoon in autumn. Signora Albini is knitting for the soldiers. Anna is reading. Lisa is running her fingers lightly over the keyboard of the piano, now and then striking a heavier chord.*

SIGNORA ALBINI.

[*Laying her work aside.*]

Well, that's enough for the present. [*To Anna, who has shut her book.*] Have you finished your book already?

ANNA.

No, not finished. But I don't feel like reading any more.

SIGNORA ALBINI.

Do you like it, though?

ANNA.

I really couldn't say. I read and read, and don't understand a word of what I'm reading. My mind's elsewhere. And your knitting?

SIGNORA ALBINI.

I'll get back to it this evening. Have you got everything ready in there?

ANNA.

All ready.

SIGNORA ALBINI.

I mean, shall we receive him there or here? Lisa, please. Stop that playing for a moment. I can't hear. . . . Very well, we'll manage things. It all depends on how much haste we'll have to make.

[*Silence.*]

ANNA.

What's the time?

LISA.

Time enough. Time enough. Don't you fear. He'll come. With military punctuality.

ANNA.

What's that got to do with it? Punctuality! He didn't specify. He simply wrote that he'd be here in the afternoon. The military punctuality is your own contribution. I was simply asking what time it was.

LISA.

[*With a faint smile.*]

You either don't remember or aren't at all aware of it, but it's the third time you've asked that question within twenty minutes. And you've also wanted to read the letter over again, to make sure that it really meant today, and that you hadn't mistaken the date. Yes, indeed. It's today. Won't you tell me why you're so impatient, and nervous?

SIGNORA ALBINI.

First explain why *you* are.

LISA.

Why *I* am?

SIGNORA ALBINI.

Yes. You want to appear calm, but you're not.

ANNA.

Good for mother!

LISA.

I, impatient and nervous? When, indeed?

SIGNORA ALBINI.

Ordinarily, no. Today, yes. You're in suspense. Just as much on edge as we. You're waiting, and whoever waits is never absolutely calm. The best you can manage is to resign yourself to a delay; but if he were not to show up, you'd suffer a terrible disappointment.

LISA.

Because he's sent word that he's coming.

SIGNORA ALBINI.

Naturally. If you didn't know that he was supposed to come . . . ! Every arrival of a new person is a proper reason for curiosity. This time it's a person that's almost unknown to us, yet dear to us just the same.

ANNA.

And add that he's young.

SIGNORA ALBINI.

Yes, but something more. Add rather that we have trembled for him. Ours isn't a vain, gossiping curiosity. It's a quivering curiosity. We have seen him only in his bandages; we know his face but little, and we have never heard him speak, so that all we have to remember him by is a timid smile.

Lisa.

That's the very reason why I can't understand the fuss you're making. I admit I'd be glad to have a look at him. But I'm not a-tremble like you.

Signora Albini.

Now don't play the brave, strong woman, **for** you deceive yourself. It's merely that your suspense shows itself differently than ours. Or rather: it was Anna who asked, "What's the time?" If *she* hadn't asked it, *you* would probably have done so. And when you resent her asking and her anxiety, it's merely another way of trying to hide your own. But you only reveal it the more.

Lisa.

Why, mother, how subtle you are!

Anna.

Mother? Always.

Signora Albini.

Hush, hush a moment. A carriage has stopped at the door. Perhaps it's he.

Lisa.

Certainly. Who else can it be? I'll take a look. [*She goes to the window.*] No. It's a lady. She's looking about, as if to make inquiries. . . .

ANNA.

[*Almost in dismay.*]

You'll see. He isn't coming, and he has sent word to let us know.

LISA.

[*Looking out.*]

She's talking with Cecchino. . . . She's at the gate. . . . She asked for us, all right. There, she's ringing.

[*Exit.*]

SIGNORA ALBINI.

It really looks as if the lieutenant at the last moment found it impossible to come. Or perhaps he's been called back to service ahead of time and he's sending us an explanation.

ANNA.

Too bad! And I wonder what's keeping that woman? I'm going to see.

[*She is about to leave when Cecchino appears on the threshold.*]

CECCHINO.

There's a lady here. She apologizes for not having a card. She gave me her name, but in a hurry, and I couldn't catch it.

SIGNORA ALBINI.

You should have asked her again.

CECCHINO.

She says that you don't know her. So that her name would have been of no use anyway.

SIGNORA ALBINI.

But just what does she want of us?

CECCHINO.

She said: "The madame . . . the young ladies. . . ." Who knows? She talks between her teeth.

LISA.

Perhaps she's a relative of his? Or maybe his wife?

ANNA.

He hasn't a wife. [*To Cecchino.*] Is she a young woman?

CECCHINO.

Yes, young. She's somewhat worn, but she seems young.

SIGNORA ALBINI.

Show her in. [*Exit Cecchino.*] We'll see. [*To Lisa, who is closing the piano.*] Tell the truth, now. Even you are anxious. You don't even try to hide it.

MARIA LÒDOLI.

[*A refined woman, dressed simply in black, enters and pauses at the door, anxiously.*]

I beg pardon. Is Lieutenant Graziani in?

SIGNORA ALBINI.

We're expecting him. He hasn't come yet.

Maria.

[Sighing deeply, her eyes sparkling.]

Ah, not yet? I feared that he might already have left. I'm sorry, I have no note of introduction, nor even a visiting card. But I had such urgent need of seeing the lieutenant! I come . . . from Piemonte. I left at daybreak. This morning I went to his house in Milan and spoke with his mother. She told me that he had left yesterday and that he would probably not be back today. And this evening I *must* return. I must. His mother told me that he would perhaps be here this afternoon, and gave me your direction. I took the train and had the presumption. . . . Please forgive me. . . . I should hate to intrude.

Signora Albini.

Don't mention it. Please come in.

Maria.

[Remaining by the door.]

I don't even know Lieutenant Graziani. *[Her hearers start with surprise.]* I am a cousin of his unfortunate flying companion — of the officer who fell with him and was killed. *[The women nod their heads sadly.]* You know all about it.

Signora Albini.

Yes, unhappily, we know. Come in, do. Don't stand there at the door like a beggar.

MARIA.

Thanks.

[*She does not move, however.*]

SIGNORA ALBINI.

Won't you sit down and rest yourself?

MARIA.

[*Takes a seat near the door.*]

SIGNORA ALBINI.

Come nearer.

MARIA.

Just let me remain here. I'll explain later.

SIGNORA ALBINI.

Your name, madame? So that I may introduce you to the lieutenant when he arrives.

MARIA.

Maria Lòdoli. The departed was a cousin to my husband. And I've come to find out certain things from the lieutenant for him. We only learned of the accident very late, ever so late. The papers said nothing. And we'd like to have some details. He had no closer relatives [*hesitating*] I believe. [*Silence.*] Lieutenant Graziani's mother told me that her son is coming to thank you for the care you gave him when he was brought here wounded. Could you perhaps tell me anything about the other one who died?

SIGNORA ALBINI.

Nothing. Almost nothing. [*Turning to Lisa and Anna.*] Nor you, either, isn't that so? The aeroplane fell within a few hundred metres of this place. . . .

MARIA.

I saw. The driver pointed the spot out to me just now, and the tree that was shattered in the fall.

SIGNORA ALBINI.

Nothing could be done for your poor cousin. He was already dead when picked up, so that they took him away and we didn't even get a look at him. Lieutenant Graziani was put up at our house because nobody thought it wise to move him about in his condition. The military physicians kept him here for a few days until they thought him strong enough to be transported to the hospital. We women took care of him. Our men — my son and my son-in-law — are at the front.

MARIA.

And Lieutenant Graziani has never spoken to you about his companion? Never asked after him?

SIGNORA ALBINI.

No, madame. While he was with us he was unable to talk. He certainly didn't know that his friend had died immediately. We told him nothing, naturally. It would only have made him worse. He must have learned of it later, at the hospital.

MARIA.

Thanks. I was . . . his only relative. My husband and I, his only relations. [*Silence.*] If I were sure that the lieutenant was delayed, say, for an hour . . . I'd go out and come back later. So as not to appear intrusive, and not be in the way. I don't want to sadden the first moments of his happy reunion with you. I'll wait in another room, if you'll be so kind. That's why I remained at the door.

SIGNORA ALBINI.

I understand. But you needn't leave. I think we can introduce you quite simply. Even without mentioning your name. "A friend of ours who happens to be visiting us." Then, when the proper moment comes, we can withdraw.

[*Lisa and Anna nod approval.*]

MARIA.

[*Weakly.*]

It's not necessary.

SIGNORA ALBINI.

But it's better. You could then ask him, and he tell you, things that aren't for strangers' ears.

MARIA.

[*Hesitant.*]

I don't know . . . I don't believe so.

SIGNORA ALBINI.

Very well. We'll see later. Don't let it trouble you. [*Introducing the women.*] My daughter, my daughter-in-law.

[*The women nod acknowledgment.*]

MARIA.

When did the accident happen?

ANNA.

The eighth of August.

MARIA.

Two months ago. I was at Alassio with my husband the whole month of September. I didn't know a thing! It was a friend of mine that told me afterwards. "Did you hear about Lòdoli?" [*Her voice trembles. Suddenly she becomes silent. To Anna and Lisa.*] You haven't any children?

ANNA.

No. Not yet. . . .

MARIA.

Oh, well, you are so young. You have time.

LISA.

And you, madame?

MARIA.

Yes.

LISA.

Already grown up?

MARIA.

Five years old.

LISA.

Just one?

MARIA.

[*Looks at her without answering. A certain
sound has made her cock her ear. It is an
automobile, which comes to a stop.*]

ANNA.

This time it's he.

LISA.

[*Runs to the window and looks out.*]

Yes, he's here. He hasn't stepped out yet, but
there's no doubt about it, for there's a soldier on the
driver's seat. That's funny! The soldier has stepped
down; the lieutenant has come out; it must be he,
but he's not in uniform. Now the soldier's getting
back into the auto and closing it.

SIGNORA ALBINI.

Poor fellow. He must be cold.

LISA.

If he'd like to warm up with a punch or some
drink . . . I'll send word to him through Cecchino.

ANNA.

We'll ask the lieutenant.

MARIA.

[*Resolutely.*]

I'm going. You can call me when you think best.
I feel that I can't face him now. I can't.

SIGNORA ALBINI.

As you see fit, madame. Go this way. [*Maria
leaves by the left; Signora Albini accompanies her, but
returns at once.*] What a strange woman!

LISA.

She's ill. You can see it at a glance, and hear it in
her voice.

LIEUTENANT GRAZIANI.

[*At the rear door, standing at attention.*]

Lieutenant Graziani.

THE WOMEN.

[*Gather around him, greeting him festively,
taking his cap.*]

Good day! Welcome! Congratulations! So glad
to see you. . . . Are you really all better?

GRAZIANI.

[*To Signora Albini.*]

You are the mother, I believe?

[*Kisses her hand.*]

SIGNORA ALBINI.

[*Smiling.*]

That's only too evident. I'm the mother and the
mother-in-law. [*Introducing.*] My daughter, my

daughter-in-law. Welcome indeed. My son and my son-in-law both wrote recently: they knew that sooner or later you'd come to see us and that it would probably be soon. So they, too, though they don't know you, send you their best regards and congratulate you from afar. Comradely greetings, for they're soldiers, too. [*With a soft sigh.*] Who isn't a soldier in these days?

Graziani.

I've come to give you the sincere and heartfelt thanks which I couldn't speak that time, but it's none the less deep and sincere for the delay. Tell the truth. Would you have recognized me? If you had come across me on the street, would you have said: "That's our wounded friend?"

Signora Albini.

[*While the other women smilingly shake their heads.*]

No, indeed! If we hadn't met you in this house, we'd never have dreamed it was you. And you, lieutenant — do you recognize us?

Graziani.

[*Looking at the three women, one after the other.*]

To tell the truth, no. At the risk of appearing an ungrateful booby, I must confess that I don't recognize you.

Signora Albini.

And how could you? We, at least, had our eyes open, while you. . . .

LISA.

Our eyes open even at night, when we watched over you.

SIGNORA ALBINI.

But your features could hardly be made out. At first all blood, and then all bandages. . . .

ANNA.

How frightful, lieutenant! Lisa, here, at least, had taken a course as a Red Cross nurse and had seen plenty of sick, wounded and dying. . . . But I. . . .

SIGNORA ALBINI.

Make yourself comfortable, lieutenant. Sit down and let's have a good look at you.

GRAZIANI.

[*Sits down, smiling, and turns toward the light.*]
So?

SIGNORA ALBINI.

Fine. That's the way. Excellent, excellent. Perfect appearance, not a trace of a scar. You were certainly lucky. And it would have been a real sin, for . . . shall I tell you? I'm an old woman and I may say it without being suspected of ulterior motives: you're a handsome young man.

LISA.

[*Smiling.*]

Oh, Oh! Mother!

ANNA.

Oh, I say, mother! Such a declaration! . . .

SIGNORA ALBINI.

What's wrong? I tell him what I'd be glad to hear said of my own son. . . . And of my son-in-law. [*Smiling.*] Yes, indeed. You are really a handsome young man. And when they carried you in here, it didn't seem. . . . Nor even afterwards: at first all blood and earth, then pale, livid, like death itself. And your mother? Tell us all about your mother. Happy, eh?

GRAZIANI.

In the seventh heaven. That is, up to yesterday. Since yesterday, not quite so happy.

SIGNORA ALBINI.

Oh!

GRAZIANI.

Because she thinks that I'm going back to flying.

SIGNORA ALBINI.

When?

GRAZIANI.

Tomorrow, or the day after.

ANNA.

Again? And so soon, after what happened to you? You're a hero.

GRAZIANI.

[*Simply.*]

No, I'm an aviator. You fall and you pick yourself up, or somebody else picks you up. You get wounded, you cure yourself, or somebody else cures you. [*Looking at his hostesses.*] And when you are in luck, it's somebody else. Then you get back on the job.

LISA.

Say rather, back to your duty.

SIGNORA ALBINI.

Look about you. Don't you remember anything? Don't you recall the place? You were carried in here, into this very room. And I didn't want to have you carried up the stairs, for they might drop you, and you in such a grave condition. For you were pretty badly off, do you know? And we women took upon ourselves a sort of duty, as if we had hurled defiance into the face of destiny: "He must be saved. We want him to be saved. Our house must prove lucky for him." Look; you were there, stretched out, first upon a mattress, then upon a cot that we had brought down. Near the piano. This is the airiest room in the house. Don't you remember a thing?

GRAZIANI.

Not a thing. Or rather . . . almost nothing. Of the first hours, certainly nothing. Then, a glimmer . . . I can't just explain it — like the shadow of a dream. And then later, a vague recollection, as of the flutter of a wing; a hand . . . [*to Signora Albini*] assuredly yours, which caressed my cheek — whatever of it there was uncovered by bandages. And a sweet feminine voice — certainly yours — that said to me: "Sleep, my boy, sleep."

SIGNORA ALBINI.

[*Moved.*]

I can't recall. It may be as you say. Won't you have something, lieutenant? Something cold or warm?

GRAZIANI.

Thank you — nothing.

ANNA.

Really? Don't stand on ceremony. Why won't you drink something? We'll drink, too, to your health.

[*Laughs.*]

GRAZIANI.

Thank you, not now. My mother wished to come in person to thank you. She will come some other day and let you know how grateful she is for the care you showed me and all the trouble you gave yourselves. . . . Today I kept her from doing so, that she might be spared the emotional strain; and also because I did not come here directly from her. I first had to make a long trip by automobile. I'm sorry, too, that I can't remain in your company as long as I should like, for there's a certain little person waiting for me.

Lisa.

Ah, ah! Congratulations!

Anna.

Excellent!

Signora Albini.

Hurrah for the lieutenant!

Graziani.

[Now understanding them.]

No, no. What did you think? A sweetheart? Not at all. Not at all. There are other things to do these days. It's another kind of little person: a fledgling sparrow.

Anna.

A sparrow?

Graziani.

[After a moment's hesitation.]

Yes, that's just what. You'll remember that when I had that fall in the test flight I wasn't alone. It was my luck that I wasn't hurt and am now on my feet, ready to begin again. The other fellow *[gravely]* Lieutenant Lòdoli, met instant death.

Lisa.

Yes, we remember. And there in the other room. . . .

Signora Albini.

[To Lisa.]

Wait, Lisa. Don't interrupt.

ANNA.

As you were saying, Lieutenant. About the unfortunate Lieutenant Lòdoli.

GRAZIANI.

Yes, a brave fellow, a serious, cultured chap. Of modest family, and had been left an orphan since boyhood — all these things I learned later. He had gone to school at Modena, lived decently and with dignity, on his wages. He was about to be promoted to a captaincy when he died. He had been a pilot for several months — a calm, certain pilot. One in a hundred fall through their own imprudence, the others fall . . . because it's their fate. I wasn't an old friend of Lòdoli. I wasn't even in his regiment or his department. I belong to the Lanciers. I had been flying only a few days. I didn't know him very well — that's why I knew almost nothing about him. And then again he was so reserved, so silent. The day before the accident happened we had spent a pretty bad moment at a high altitude because of an injury to the motor. When we landed I said: "Do you realize that we just had a narrow escape?" And he answered: "Yes. And I felt bad on account of the little sparrow." Nothing more. He said not a word more, nor did I ask him anything else. The little sparrow? It occurred to me an hour later, but then . . . The next day — well, you know what happened. . . . When I was already convalescing they showed me the wallet that they had found in his jacket; naturally it hadn't yet been touched. No

will, no money to speak of — just a few tens and
some notes of little importance. But in the inner-
most pocket there was a photograph of a two-year-
old child; on the back of the photograph, the name,
Giulio Lòdoli, the place and date of birth and exact
directions for finding him: "With the Piombesi
family, Cascina Grossa, Gallarate."

ANNA.

[*In a low voice.*]

The little sparrow.

GRAZIANI.

I thought of the little fellow, then I wrote. I went
to Gallarate at once, and we returned this morning.
The Piombesis are fine folk, but poor country people.
They are fond of the little one, but even more fond
of the little income that he meant to them. For
every month, punctually, Lieutenant Lòdoli would
send to Maddalena Piombesi sixty *lire* of his pay,
to cover the nurse's wages and the maintenance of
the child. And whenever he could, he took a run
out to see his child. Poor little thing! I've seen him;
he's a husky little dear. Nobody's yet come to hunt
him out; times are hard. So I took him.

SIGNORA ALBINI.

You took him?

GRAZIANI.

For my mother more than for myself. It's a kind
deed and at the same time it will gladden my old

mother's heart. I'm a bachelor, and an only son; my mother's alone; the child will keep her company.

SIGNORA ALBINI.

And if it's called for?

GRAZIANI.

The Piombesis know who I am and where I belong. If anybody shows up with a right to the child, we'll talk the matter over and see. In the meantime it's with me. It's outside, in the automobile.

LISA.

Outside? With whom?

GRAZIANI.

My attendant is taking good care of him.

SIGNORA ALBINI.

But the mother? What will the mother say?

GRAZIANI.

What mother? Mine? She'll say, "Welcome." And she'll keep him.

SIGNORA ALBINI.

Have you spoken to her about it? Does she know that you're not coming back alone?

GRAZIANI.

No. It's a surprise. Just a little sparrow found shivering in the grass, exposed to the weather, and brought home to warmth, food and care.

LIŞA.

But the mother? The little one's mother? Didn't you ask the Piombesi family whether the mother had ever come to see the child? . . . Who she was?

GRAZIANI.

Lieutenant Lòdoli was a bachelor. As for near relatives — none! There aren't any other Lòdolis at Ivrea. The Lòdolis come from Ivrea.

LISA.

But the little fellow had a mother.

> [*Maria Lòdoli appears. Signora Albini approaches so as to bring her forward. Maria Lòdoli signals her not to speak nor to interrupt the lieutenant, who goes on with his story.*]

GRAZIANI.

Who the mother is? Perhaps we ought to ask ourselves who *was* the mother. She may be dead. Lòdoli never said a word about her to any of his comrades. The Piombesi family knows nothing of her — never saw her. The child was brought to them by Lieutenant Lòdoli, who was accompanied by a young lady from Varese. Should I hunt for this woman at Varese? Would I be able to find her? And would she, could she, talk? And — perhaps — it's better not to know. We officers wander about the world, here today, there tomorrow — we visit so many cities, in garrison and in detachment! It can't be a woman who is free to act, for she would have taken the child, or at least have looked it up. It can hardly be a woman of the upper classes. No. It's probably some waitress or a teacher, to whom the child would prove a disaster in the first place and a hindrance later on. More likely the latter, for Lieutenant Lòdoli, if only for the child's sake, would have made reparation by marrying the mother. The mother's probably some low, shameless person. Let's do nothing about it; let's make no search, for it isn't worth while. I'll take the child without any hesitation. And when he grows up: "Giulio Lòdoli, son of an officer in the aviation corps who died in service." That's reason enough to hold one's head high, don't you think?

> [*As he speaks thus, he turns his eyes to Maria Lòdoli, who has shrunk back, mute, pale, rigid. An "Oh!" escapes her lips, betokening intense surprise. She is fairly transfixed with suspense.*]

Signora Albini.

My dear lieutenant, we didn't speak of it before, so as not to disturb you, and also because we were requested not to. This lady came here to speak with you; she's Lieutenant Lòdoli's cousin. [*Graziani nods acknowledgment.*] Your mother told her that you would be here. She wished to get news from you about Lòdoli's death — some of the details. We don't know just what. We'll leave her with you.

> [*With her eyes rather than with her hands, Signora Albini signals Anna and Lisa to*

*leave. They do so silently. Signora Albini
follows them, and very softly closes the door.
Maria Lòdoli, as if petrified, seems to have
lost sight, voice, the power to move. A pro-
longed silence. Then, without stirring,
Maria Lòdoli breaks the quiet, in a low voice,
almost in a single breath.*]

MARIA.

It's I. I'm the mother. I'm little Giulio's mother.

GRAZIANI.

[*Astounded.*]

You? !

MARIA.

I. I'm not the dead man's cousin. I'm not the one
I said I was. My name is not Maria Lòdoli. It's
something else. Don't ask. Yes, yes. Do take the
child with you; take it to your mother. Don't leave
it in other hands: mercenary hands, or too delicate
ones. Among poor folks he would be a burden, and
among rich he would be a mere plaything, a puppy.
You're a friend of his father's. You're altogether
different. Is he handsome? Tell me. He was so
handsome! Just imagine, I have scarcely seen him.
When he was but a few days old he was taken away
from me. I never saw him again.

GRAZIANI.

Why?

MARIA.

Don't ask. I couldn't. What those years have
cost me! I couldn't. [*In despair.*] I have a husband
. . . and another child — his, my husband's. I
couldn't. Confess? Who confesses without hope of
pardon? Leave my husband? That would be a
worse infamy. He is so good! He doesn't suspect a
thing. He would be prostrated. And then there's
another — my other little one. I can't leave him.
He's five years old. To reclaim this one would be to
lose the other. My husband would have to be a
saint to receive the other. And then people — what
would people say? Not about me. What do I care
about myself? But about him? About my husband?
Ah! Why is one so weak against temptation? My
husband was in America; he, the poor departed, was
a friend of my girlhood days. . . . He visited the
house. . . . He was young, much younger than I
. . . he had no other ties. . . . And the other was
so far away — had been, for a year. A tiny town,
with no amusements, nothing to occupy one's mind.
It's the same old story. I was secluded for four
months. Nobody knew. I was cared for in a hospital . . . long illness . . . grave anemia. Nobody
knew. There. I had told you not to ask, and now
you know everything from my own lips. But you're
a soldier. You'll keep it to yourself. He's a handsome little boy? My child is a sweet dear?

GRAZIANI.

A handsome little chap.

Maria.

Blond? He was blond when he was born. April 10, 1914. You see, I remember. He has an old gold medallion [*the lieutenant nods affirmatively*]. You see, I know. That was given to me by my poor dead mother when I was still a child. It must be around his neck. It's on his neck, isn't it?

Graziani.

Would you like to see him? Would you like to have a look at your little boy?

Maria.

[*Resolutely, almost harshly.*]

No.

Graziani.

[*Amazed.*]

No? Why? He's down in the automobile. I'll fetch him at once, well wrapped.

Maria.

No. If I have a look at him, I'll be unable to tear myself away. And the other one's waiting for me. No. Please ask your mother to have him say a few words for me in his evening prayers. Your mother must be so kind! A mere glance into her face was enough to reveal that. Let her be indulgent toward me; let her feel pity. I have sinned; but I've paid for it and I'm paying. It consumes me. Anemia — they think it's anemia! And I force myself to keep up the deception, for the sake of my other little one, and for my poor husband. . . . What a life!

GRAZIANI.

I understand. I understand.

MARIA.

And you, you. How will you have my little boy
call you?

GRAZIANI.

Uncle. I'll be the uncle.

MARIA.

Ah! He already calls you that, does he? Tell me.
Do. And your mother — how will he call your
mother? Not mamma, no. Not mamma. Granny.
Let him call her granny! Kiss her hands for me. . . .
Kiss her hands for me. For me.

[*A loud clamor of feminine voices is heard from
within.*]

VOICES.

Here he is. How handsome! What a dear! Just
see him smile!

[*Maria Lòdoli withdraws to the rear, pale and
excited. Anna enters, triumphantly bearing
aloft in her arms a little fellow not much more
than two years old, wrapped in a cover: it is
the little sparrow.*]

ANNA.

[*To Graziani.*]

Lieutenant, we simply couldn't resist the temptation. We wanted so much to see him. He was awake.

We took him in. A biscuit for the little fellow? May we give him a biscuit? Yes? [*Then, looking about.*] And Madame Lòdoli?

[*Maria Lòdoli has disappeared.*]

CURTAIN.

LUIGI PIRANDELLO

(1867–

Luigi Pirandello was born on June 28, 1867 at Girgenti, Sicily. After a thorough education in Italy he went to the University of Bonn, where he was graduated in philosophy and philology. His subsequent career has been devoted to professorship, but has permitted him enough leisure in which to produce a veritable library of books, covering a wide range and revealing a fine quality.

From poetry he progressed to the novel, to criticism, to the theatre. Indeed, his novel "Il Fu Mattia Pascal" (1904), which has been translated into French and German, is one of the most original Italian books of the twentieth century and was responsible for his stepping beyond the national frontier. It is written in a witty, fluent, Boccaccesque style, in which the author reveals his characteristic capability of treating humorously situations of underlying seriousness. In his fiction he has been called a "gay pessimist" — a sobriquet that seems to match his paradoxical style with a corresponding paradox; his pessimism, however, is found not to be the Anglo-Saxon type, for underneath it seems to flow a current of faith. The man's writings are really topsy-turvy, compounded of cynicism jostling against sentimentality, Christian self-abnegation rubbing elbows with anarchic denial. Pirandello is an "intellectual." One suspects in him the man whose emotions and intellect never have reached a state of stable equilibrium; now one, now the other, is uppermost, with a resultant kaleidoscope of many-colored notions, ideas, feelings, reactions.

He has been credited with having brought to the stage his own peculiar humorism, upon which, by the way, he has written a tightly packed volume, and he is no small asset to the "grotesque" movement. An American critic has written that his work for the theatre lacks the "modern" tinge, yet he is peculiarly a symptom of modernity struggling to acclimate itself upon the Italian "boards." He is no stranger to the plays of Ibsen, Shaw, Bracco. And if he began with the bitter-sweet little piece by which he is represented in this collection, he has since done things that single him out for sheer daring and originality. Among his numerous plays perhaps "Così e (se vi pare) — It's So, If You Think It is — best shows him in his puzzling, paradoxical mood, even as "Se non così" (If Not Thus) gives his best measure as a dramatist of social change. The first of these is a swiftly moving three-act comedy designed to suggest, as the title hints, that the truth is hardly so easy to grasp as some would imagine. Perhaps there is more than one truth; perhaps when people contradict each other they are both right; is there such a thing as truth at all? Is Truth a Delphic oracle? And what a strange, silly sight we present chasing after it with more of the inquisitive gossip in us than that of the sober searcher after any real good! The action is, up to the somewhat disconcerting close, quite breathless, and the story is followed with amused bepuzzlement. The second of the plays presents a strange twist to the eternal triangle, in which the child begotten by the erring husband and his mistress is the crux of the situation. For, curiously enough, the wronged wife wishes to bring up the child as her own; but so does the real mother, who is willing enough to have the husband return to the hearth whence he strayed. Admitting the plausability of the wife's views, the play is strong, dignified and moving. There is little drama in the conventional sense, despite some affecting scenes in the second and third acts. The action lies mainly in the working out of the wife's views and the dialogue that arises from the exposition of them.

Pirandello, like most of the leading Italians, writes too much. His best, however, is so plainly expressive of a decidedly arresting personality that it will remain as one of the traits of contemporary Italian belles-lettres.

PERSONS

MICUCCIO BONAVINO, *musician in a country band.*

MARTA MARNIS, *mother of*

SINA MARNIS, *singer.*

FERDINANDO, *waiter.*

DORINA, *maid.*

GUESTS.

WAITERS.

TIME: The present.   PLACE: A city in Northern Italy.

SICILIAN LIMES

SCENE: *A hallway, furnished simply with a small table and several chairs. The corner to the left of the actors is hidden from view by a curtain. There are doors at the right and the left. At the rear, the main door, of glass, is open and leads to a dark room across which may be seen a decorated door, likewise of glass, which affords a view of a splendidly illuminated salon. The view includes a table, sumptuously spread.*

NIGHT. *The hallway is in darkness. Some one is snoring behind the curtain.*

Shortly after the rise of the stage curtain Ferdinando enters through the door at the right with a light in his hand. He is in shirt sleeves, but he has only to put on his dress-coat and he will be ready to serve at the table. He is followed by Micuccio Bonavino, evidently just from the country, with his overcoat collar raised to his ears, a grimy bag in one hand and in the other an old valise and the case of a musical instrument. He is so cold and so exhausted that he can barely manage his burden. No sooner has the light been brought in than the snoring behind the curtain ceases.

DORINA.

[*From within.*]

Who is it?

FERDINANDO.

[*Placing the light upon the little table.*]

Hey, Dorina! Get up! Can't you see that we have Signor Bonvicino here?

MICUCCIO.

[*Shaking his head so as to get rid of a drop at the tip of his nose.*]

My name's Bonavino.

FERDINANDO.

Bonavino, Bonavino.

DORINA.

[*Yawning behind the curtain.*]

And who's he?

FERDINANDO.

A relation of madame's. [*To Micuccio.*] And just how may you be related to madame, please? Cousin, maybe?

MICUCCIO.

[*Embarrassed, hesitant.*]

Well, really, there's no relationship. I am . . . my name's Micuccio Bonavino. You know that.

DORINA.

[*Her curiosity roused, she steps from behind the curtain, still half asleep.*]

A relative of madame's?

FERDINANDO.

[*Provoked.*]

Can't you hear? [*To Micuccio.*] Countryman of hers? Then why did you ask me whether *zia* Marta was here? [*To Dorina.*] Understand? I took him for a relative, a nephew. I can't receive you, my dear fellow.

MICUCCIO.

What? Can't receive me? Why, I've come all the way from the country, on purpose!

FERDINANDO.

On purpose? What for?

MICUCCIO.

To find her!

FERDINANDO.

She's not here. I told you she can't be found in at this hour.

MICUCCIO.

And if the train just came in, what can I do about it? I've been traveling for two days.

DORINA.

[*Eyeing him from head to toe.*]

And you look it!

MICUCCIO.

I do, eh? Very much? How do I look?

DORINA.

Ugly, my dear fellow. No offense.

FERDINANDO.

I can't receive you. Call again tomorrow and you'll find her. The madame is at the theatre now.

MICUCCIO.

What do you mean, call again? Must I go? Where? I don't know where to go in this town, at night. I'm a stranger. If she isn't here, I'll wait for her. Really now. Can't I wait for her here?

FERDINANDO.

I say No! Without her permission.

MICUCCIO.

What permission! You don't know me.

FERDINANDO.

That's just it. Because I don't know you, I'm not going to get a bawling-out on account of you!

MICUCCIO.

[*Smiling with a confident air and with his finger making a negative sign.*]

Rest easy.

DORINA.

[*To Ferdinando, ironically.*]

Indeed, she'll be just in the proper mood to attend to him this evening. [*To Micuccio.*] Can't you see? [*She points to the illuminated salon in the rear.*] There's a party on tonight!

MICUCCIO.

So? What party?

DORINA.

An evening in [*she yawns*] her honor.

FERDINANDO.

And we'll get through, God willing, by daybreak!

MICUCCIO.

All right, no matter. I'm sure that the moment
Teresina sees me. . .

FERDINANDO.

[*To Dorina.*]

Understand? He calls her Teresina, he does.
Plain Teresina. He asked me whether "Teresina,
the singer" was in.

MICUCCIO.

Well, what of it? Isn't she a singer? That's what
they call it. Are you trying to teach *me?*

DORINA.

Then you really know her well?

MICUCCIO.

Well? Why, we grew up together!

FERDINANDO.

[*To Dorina.*]

What shall we do?

DORINA.

Let him wait.

MICUCCIO.

[*Piqued.*]

Of course I'll wait. What do you mean? I came
on purpose to . . .

FERDINANDO.

Take a seat there. I wash my hands of it. I must get things ready. [*He leaves in the direction of the salon at the rear.*]

MICUCCIO.

This is fine, indeed. As if I were . . . Perhaps because they see me in this condition . . . If I were to tell Teresina when she returns from the theatre. [*He is seized by a doubt and looks about him.*] Whose house is this?

DORINA.

[*Eyeing him and poking fun at him.*]
Ours — as long as we stay.

MICUCCIO.

So, then, things are going well. [*He inspects the place anew, staring into the salon.*] Is it a large house?

DORINA.

So so.

MICUCCIO.

And that's a salon?

DORINA.

A reception hall. Tonight there's a banquet there.

MICUCCIO.

Ah! What a spread! What bright lights!

DORINA.

Beautiful, isn't it?

MICUCCIO.

[*Rubbing his hands contentedly.*]

Then it's true!

DORINA.

What?

MICUCCIO.

Eh, it's easily seen, they're well. . .

DORINA.

In good health?

MICUCCIO.

No, I mean well off. [*He rubs his thumb against his forefinger, in a manner to suggest the counting of money.*]

DORINA.

Why, do you know who Sina Marnis is?

MICUCCIO.

Sina? Ah, yes, yes, now I understand. *Zia* Marta wrote me about it. Teresina. Certainly. Tere-sina: Sina. . .

DORINA.

But wait a moment. Now that I think of it. You [*She calls Ferdinando from the salon.*] Do you know who he is? The fellow that she's always writing to, the mother . . .

MICUCCIO.

She can't write, the poor little thing . . .

DORINA.

Yes, yes. Bonavino. But . . . Domenico. Your name's Domenico, isn't it?

MICUCCIO.

Domenico or Micuccio. It's the same thing. We call it Micuccio where I come from.

DORINA.

You're the fellow that was so sick, aren't you? Recently . . .

MICUCCIO.

Terribly, yes. At death's door. Dead. Practically dead.

DORINA.

And Signora Marta sent you a money order, didn't she? We went to the post-office together.

MICUCCIO.

A money order. A money order. And that's what I've come for! I have it here — the money.

DORINA.

Are you returning it to her?

MICUCCIO.

[*Disturbed.*]

Money — nothing! It's not to be mentioned. But first . . . Will they be much longer in coming?

DORINA.

[*Looks at the clock.*]

Oh, about . . . Sometime tonight, I imagine . . .

FERDINANDO.

[*Passing through the hallway, from the door at
the left, carrying kitchen utensils and shouting
applause.*]

Bravo! Bravo! Bis! Bis! Bis!

MICUCCIO.

[*Smiling.*]

A great voice, eh?

FERDINANDO.

[*Turning back.*]

I should say so. A voice. . .

MICUCCIO.

[*Rubbing his palms.*]

I can take the credit for that! It's my work!

DORINA.

Her voice?

MICUCCIO.

I discovered it!

DORINA.

What, you? [*To Ferdinando.*] Do you hear? He
discovered her voice.

MICUCCIO.

I'm a musician, I am.

FERDINANDO.

Ah! A musician? Bravo! And what do you play?
The trumpet?

MICUCCIO.

[*At first, in all seriousness, makes a negative sign with his finger; then*]

Who said trumpet? The piccolo. I belong to the band, I do. I belong to our communal band up at my place.

DORINA.

And what's the name of your place? Wait; I'll recall it.

MICUCCIO.

Palma Monetchiaro. What else should it be named?

FERDINANDO.

And it was really you who discovered her voice?

DORINA.

Come now, my boy. Tell us how you did it, sonny! Wait and listen to this, Ferdinando.

MICUCCIO.

[*Shrugging his shoulders.*]

How I did it? She used to sing . . .

DORINA.

And at once, you being a musician . . . eh?

MICUCCIO.

No . . . not at once; on the other hand . . .

FERDINANDO.

It took you some time?

Micuccio.

She always used to be singing . . . sometimes out of pique. . .

Dorina.

Really?

Micuccio.

And then again, to . . . to get certain thoughts out of her mind . . . because . . .

Ferdinando.

Because what?

Micuccio.

Oh, certain unpleasant things . . . disappointments, poor little girl . . . in those days. Her father had died. . . I,— yes, I helped her out a bit . . . her and her mother, *zia* Marta. . . But my mother was against it . . . and . . . in short . . .

Dorina.

You were fond of her, then?

Micuccio.

I? Of Teresina? You make me laugh! My mother insisted on my giving her up because she didn't have anything, and had lost her father . . . while I, come good or evil, had my position in the band. . .

Ferdinando.

So . . . You're not related at all, then. Lovers, maybe?

MICUCCIO.

My parents were against it! And that's why
Teresina sang out of spite. . .

DORINA.

Ah! Just listen to that. . . And you?

MICUCCIO.

It was heaven! I can truly say: an inspiration
from heaven! Nobody had ever noticed it — not
even I. All of a sudden . . . one morning . . .

FERDINANDO.

There's luck for you!

MICUCCIO.

I'll never forget it. . . It was a morning in April.
She was at the window, singing. . . Up in the garret,
beneath the roof!

FERDINANDO.

Understand?

DORINA.

Hush!

MICUCCIO.

What's wrong about that? The humblest of folk
can have the greatest of gifts.

DORINA.

Of course they can! As you were saying? She was
at the window singing. . .

MICUCCIO.

I had heard her sing that little air of ours surely
a hundred thousand times.

DORINA.

Little air?

MICUCCIO.

Yes. "All things in this world below." That's the name of it.

FERDINANDO.

Eh! All things in this world below. . .

MICUCCIO.

[*Reciting the words.*]

All things in this world below,
Live their day and then depart;
But this thorn that pricks my heart,
Darling mine, will never go.

And what a melody! Divine, impassioned. . . Enough of that. I had never paid any attention to it. But that morning. . . It was as if I were in paradise! An angel, it seemed that an angel was singing! That day, after dinner, ever so quietly, without letting her or her mother know a thing about it, I took up into the garret the leader of our band, who's a friend of mine, uh, a very close friend, for that matter: Saro Malvati, such a kind-hearted chap, the poor fellow. . . He hears her, he's a clever boy, a great leader, so they all say at Palma. . . And he says, "Why, this is a God-given voice!" Imagine our joy! I hired a piano, and before it was got up into that attic. . . Well. Then I bought the music, and right away the leader began to give her lessons. . . Just like that, satisfied with whatever they could give him from time to time. What was I? Same as I am today; a poor, humble fellow. . . The piano cost money, the music cost money, and then Teresina had to eat decent food. . .

FERDINANDO.

Eh, of course.

DORINA.

So that she's had the strength to sing. . .

MICUCCIO.

Meat, every day! I can take the credit for that!

FERDINANDO.

The deuce you say!

DORINA.

And so?

MICUCCIO.

And so she began to learn. You could see it all from the very beginning. . . It was written above, in heaven, you might say. . . And it was heard throughout the whole country, that great voice of hers. . . The people would come from all around, and stand beneath the window in the street, to hear her. . . And what spirit! She burned, she really was afire. . . And when she would finish singing, she'd grasp me by the arm, like this [*he seizes Ferdinando*] and would shake me. . . Just like a madwoman. . . For she already foresaw. She knew that fame was hers. . . The leader told us so. And she didn't know how to show me her gratefulness. *Zia* Marta, on the other hand, poor woman that she was . . .

DORINA.

Was against her career?

MICUCCIO.

I wouldn't say that she was against it — she didn't believe it, that was it. The poor old lady had had so many hard knocks in her life that she didn't want Teresina to take it into her head to rise above the position to which she had been so long resigned. She was, in plain words, afraid. And then she knew what it cost me, and that my parents. . . But I broke with them all, with my father, with my mother, when a certain teacher came from outside. . . He used to give concerts. . . A. . . I can't remember his name now — but he had a fine reputation. . . When this master heard Teresina and said that it would be a sin, a real sin not to have her continue her studies in a city, in a great conservatory . . . I broke with them all. I sold the farm that had been left to me by an uncle of mine, a priest, and sent Teresina to Naples.

FERDINANDO.

You?

MICUCCIO.

Yes, I.—I.

DORINA.

[*To Ferdinando.*]

At his expense, don't you understand?

MICUCCIO.

I kept her there for four years, studying. I haven't
seen her since then.

DORINA.

Never?

MICUCCIO.

Never. Because . . . because she began to sing
in the theatres, you see, here and there. . . She'd
fly from Naples to Rome, from Rome to Milan, then
to Spain, then to Russia, then back here again. . .

FERDINANDO.

Creating a furore everywhere!

Eh, I know all about it! I've got them all here,
in the valise, all the papers. . . And in here [*he
removed from his inside coat pocket a bundle of letters.*]
I have all the letters, hers and her mother's. . .
Here you are: these are her words when she sent me
the money, that time I was on the point of death:
"Dear Micuccio, I haven't time to write to you.
I confirm everything that mamma has said. Get
better at once, become your old self again, and wish
me well. Teresina."

FERDINANDO

And did she send you much?

DORINA.

A thousand lire — wasn't it?

MICUCCIO.

That was it. A thousand.

FERDINANDO.

And that farm of yours, if I may ask — that you sold. How much was it worth?

MICUCCIO.

How much should it be worth? Not much . . . A mere strip of land. . .

FERDINANDO.

[*Winking to Dorina.*]

Ah!

MICUCCIO.

But I have the money right here, I have. I don't want anything at all. What little I've done, I've done for her sake. We had agreed to wait two, three years, so as to let her make a place for herself. . . *Zia* Marta kept writing that to me all the time in her letters. I speak the plain truth: I wasn't waiting for the money. So many years had passed I could wait a while longer. . . But seeing that Teresina has sent it to me, it's a sign she has enough and to spare; she's made a place for herself. . .

FERDINANDO.

I should say! And what a place, my dear sir!

MICUCCIO.

Then it's time . . .

DORINA.

To marry?

MICUCCIO.

I am here.

FERDINANDO.

Have you come to marry Sina Marnis?

DORINA.

Hush! That's their agreement! Can't you understand anything? Certainly! To marry her!

MICUCCIO.

I'm not saying anything. I simply say: I'm here.
I've abandoned everything and everybody yonder
in the country: family, band, everything. I went
to law against my parents on account of those
thousand lire, which came unknown to me, at the
time I was more dead than alive. I had to tear it
out of my mother's hands, for she wanted to keep it.
Ah, no sirree — it isn't the money! Micuccio Bonavino, money? — Not at all! Wherever I may happen
to be, even at the end of the world, I won't starve.
I have my art. I have my piccolo, and . . .

DORINA.

You have? Did you bring along your piccolo, too?

MICUCCIO.

Sure I did! We're as one person, my piccolo and
I. . .

FERDINANDO.

She sings and he plays. Understand?

MICUCCIO.

Don't you think I can play in the orchestra?

FERDINANDO.

Certainly! Why not?

DORINA.

And, I'll bet you play well!

MICUCCIO.

So so; I've been playing for ten years. . .

FERDINANDO.

Would you mind letting us hear something?
[*About to take the instrument case.*]

DORINA.

Yes! Bravo, bravo! Let's hear something!

MICUCCIO.

Oh, no! What would you want, at this hour. . .

DORINA.

Anything at all! Please, now!

FERDINANDO.

Some little air. . .

MICUCCIO.

Oh, no. . . Really! . . .

FERDINANDO.

Don't make us coax you! [*He opens the case and removes the instrument.*] Here you are!

DORINA.

Come, now. Let's hear something. . .

MICUCCIO.

But, really, it's impossible. . . Like this —
alone. . .

DORINA.

No matter! Come on. Make a try!

FERDINANDO.

If you don't, I'll play the thing!

MICUCCIO.

For me, if you wish. . . Shall I play for you the
air that Teresina sang that day, up in the garret?

FERDINANDO AND DORINA.

Yes, yes! Bravo! Bravo!

FERDINANDO.

"All things in this world below"?

MICUCCIO.

All things in this world below.

[*Micuccio sits down and begins to play in all
seriousness. Ferdinando and Dorina do
their best to keep from bursting into laughter.
The other waiter, in dress coat, comes in to
listen, followed by the cook and the scullion.
Ferdinando and Dorina caution them by signs
to listen quietly and earnestly. Micuccio's
playing is suddenly interrupted by a loud
ringing of the bell.*]

FERDINANDO.

Oh! Here's madame!

DORINA.

> [*To the other waiters.*]

Be off, now. Open the door. [*To the cook and the scullion.*] And you, clear out! She said she wanted to have dinner served as soon as she came back.

> [*The other waiter, the cook and the scullion leave.*]

FERDINANDO.

My dress coat. . . Where did I put it?

DORINA.

There! [*She points to behind the hangings and leaves in haste.*]

> [*Micuccio arises, his instrument in his hand, abashed. Ferdinando finds his coat, puts it on hurriedly, then, seeing that Micuccio is about to follow Dorina, stops him rudely.*]

FERDINANDO.

You stay here! I must first let madame know.

> [*Ferdinando leaves. Micuccio is left in dejection, confused, oppressed by an uneasy presentiment.*]

MARTA'S VOICE.

> [*From within.*]

In there, Dorina! In the drawing room!

> [*Ferdinando, Dorina and the other waiter enter from the door at the right and cross the stage toward the salon in the background, carrying magnificent baskets of flowers, wreaths, and so on. Micuccio sticks his head forward to*]

get a look into the salon and catches sight of
a large number of gentlemen, all in evening
dress, conversing confusedly. Dorina returns
in a great hurry, hastening to the door at
the right.]

MICUCCIO.

[Touching her arm.]

Who are they?

DORINA.

[Without stopping.]

The guests! [Exit.]

[Micuccio stares again. His vision becomes
clouded. His stupefaction and his commotion
are so great that he himself does not realize
that his eyes are moist with tears. He closes
them, pulls himself together, as if to resist
the torture inflicted upon him by a shrill
outburst of laughter. It is Sina Marnis, in
the salon. Dorina returns with two more
baskets of flowers.]

DORINA.

[Without stopping, hastening toward the salon.]
What are you crying about?

MICUCCIO.

I? . . . No. . . All those people . . .

[Enter ZIA Marta from the door at the right.
The poor old lady is oppressed by a hat and a
costly, splendid velvet cloak. As soon as she
sees Micuccio she utters a cry that is at once
suppressed.]

MARTA.

What! Micuccio, you here?

MICUCCIO.

[*Uncovering his face and staring at her almost in fear.*]

Zia Marta! Good Lord. . . Like this? You?

MARTA.

Why, what's wrong with me?

MICUCCIO.

With a hat? You!

MARTA.

Ah. . . [*Shakes her head and raises her hand. Then, disturbed.*] But how on earth did you come? Without a word of warning! How did it happen?

MICUCCIO.

I . . . I came . . .

MARTA.

And this evening, of all others! Oh, heavens. . . Wait. . . What shall I do? What shall I do? Do you see how many people we have here, my son? Tonight is the party in honor of Teresina. . .

MICUCCIO.

I know.

MARTA.

Her special evening, understand? Wait. . . Just wait here a moment. . .

MICUCCIO.

If you, if you think that it would be best for me
to go. . .

MARTA.

No. Wait a moment, I say. . .. [*She goes off
toward the salon.*]

MICUCCIO.

I wouldn't know where to go. . . In this strange
city. . .

> [*ZIA Marta returns, and signals him with her
> gloved hand to wait. She enters the salon and
> suddenly there is a deep silence. There are
> heard clearly these words of Sina Marnis:
> "A moment, my friends!" Micuccio again
> hides his face in his hands. But Sina does
> not come. Instead, ZIA Marta enters shortly
> afterward, without her hat, without her gloves,
> without her cloak, now less burdened.*]

MARTA.

Here I am. . . Here I am. . .

MICUCCIO.

And . . . and Teresina?

MARTA.

I've told her. . . I've brought her the news. . .
As soon as . . . as soon as she can get a moment,
she'll come. . . In the meantime we'll stay here a
little while, eh? Are you satisfied?

MICUCCIO.

As far as I'm concerned. . .

MARTA.

I'll keep you company. . .

MICUCCIO.

Oh, no, . . . if . . . if you'd rather . . . that
is, if you're needed there. . .

MARTA.

Not at all. . . They're having supper now, see?
Admirers of hers. . . The impresario. . . Her career,
understand? We two will stay here. Dorina will
prepare this little table for us right away, and . . .
and we'll have supper together, just you and I, here—
eh? What do you say? We two, all alone — eh?
We'll recall the good old times. . . [*Dorina returns
through the door at the left with a tablecloth and other
articles of the table service.*]

MARTA.

Come on, Dorina. . . Lively, now. . . For me
and for this dear boy of mine. My dear Micuccio!
I can't believe that we're together again.

DORINA.

Here. In the meantime, please be seated.

MARTA.

[*Sitting down.*]

Yes, yes. . . Here, like this, apart from the others,
we two alone. . . In there, you understand, so
many people. . . She, poor thing, can't very well

leave them. . . Her career. . . What else can she
do? Have you seen the papers? Wonderful happen-
ings, my boy! And as for me, I'm all in a whirl. . .
It seems impossible that I should be sitting here alone
with you tonight. . . [*She rubs her hands and smiles,
gazing at him through tender eyes.*]

MICUCCIO.

[*In a pensive, anguished voice.*]
And, she'll come? She told you she'd come? I
mean . . . just to get a look at her, at least. . .

MARTA.

Of course she'll come! As soon as she can find a
moment to spare. Didn't I tell you so? Why, just
imagine what pleasure it would be for her to be here
with us, with you, after such a long time. . . How
many years is it? So many, so many. . . Ah, my
dear boy, it seems an eternity to me. . . How many
things I've been through, things that . . . that hardly
seem true when I think of them. . . Who could have
imagined, when . . . when we were yonder in Palma
when you used to come up into our garret, with its
swallows' nests in the rafters, remember? They
used to fly all over the house, and my beautiful
pots of basil on the window-sill. . . And donna
Annuzza, donna Annuzza? Our old neighbor?

MICUCCIO.

Eh. . . [*Makes the sign of benediction with two
fingers, to signify, Dead!*]

MARTA.

Dead? Yes, I imagined so. . . She was a pretty old lady even then. . . Older than I. . . Poor donna Annunzza, with her clove of garlic. . . Do you remember? She'd always come with that pretext, a clove of garlic. Just when we were about to send her down a bite, and . . . The poor old lady! And who knows how many more have passed on eh? at Palma. . . Ah! At least they rest yonder, in their last sleep, in our churchyard, with their beloved ones and relatives. . . While I. . . Who knows where I'll leave these bones of mine? Enough of that. . . Away with such thoughts! [*Dorina enters with the first course and stands beside Micuccio, waiting for him to help himself.*] Ah, here's Dorina. . .

MICUCCIO.

[*Looks at Dorina, then at ZIA Marta, confused, perplexed; he raises his hand to help himself, sees that they are grimy from the journey and lowers them, more confused than ever.*]

MARTA.

Here, over here, Dorina! I'll serve him. . . Leave it to me. . . [*Does so.*] There. . . That's fine, isn't it?

MICUCCIO.

Oh, yes . . . Thanks .

MARTA.

[*Who has served herself.*]

Here you are . . .

MICUCCIO.

[*Winking, and with his closed fist against his cheek making a gesture of ecstatic approval.*]
Uhm . . . Good . . . Good stuff.

MARTA.

A special honor-evening . . . Understand? To it, now! Let's eat! But first . . . [*She makes the sign of the cross.*] Here I can do it, in your company.

MICUCCIO.

[*Likewise makes the sign of the cross.*]

MARTA.

Bravo, my boy! You, too . . . Bravo, my Micuccio, the same as ever, poor fellow! Believe me . . . When I have to eat in there . . . without being able to cross myself . . . it seems to me that the food can't go down . . . Eat, eat!

MICUCCIO.

Eh, I'm good and hungry, I am! I . . . I haven't eaten for two days.

MARTA.

What do you mean? On the trip?

MICUCCIO.

I took plenty to eat along with me . . . I have it there, in the valise. But . . .

MARTA.

But what?

Micuccio.

I . . . I was ashamed . . . It . . . it seemed so little . . .

Marta.

Oh, how silly! . . . Come, now. . . Eat, my poor Micuccio. . . You certainly must be famished! Two days . . . And drink . . . here, drink . . . [*She pours some liquor for him.*]

Micuccio.

Thanks . . . Yes, I'll have some . . .

[*From time to time, as the two waiters enter the salon in the background or leave it with the courses, opening the door, there comes from inside a wave of confused words and outbursts of laughter. Micuccio raises his head from his plate, disturbed, and looks into the sorrowful affectionate eyes of ZIA Marta, as if to read in them an explanation of it all.*]

They're laughing.

Marta.

Yes . . . Drink . . . Drink . . . Ah, that good old wine of ours, Micuccio. If you only knew how how I long for it! The wine Michela used to make, Michela, who lived underneath us . . . What's become of Michela, my son?

Micuccio.

Michela? Oh, she's fine. She's fine.

MARTA.

And her daughter Luzza?

MICUCCIO.

She's married . . . Has two children already. . . .

MARTA.

Is that so? Really? She'd always come up to us, remember? Such a happy nature, too! Oh, Luzza. And to think of it . . . Just to think of it . . . Married . . . And whom did she marry?

MICUCCIO.

Toto Licasi, the fellow that worked in the customs house. Remember him?

MARTA.

Him? Fine . . . And donna Mariangela is a grandmother! A grandmother already . . . Fortunate woman! Two children, did you say?

MICUCCIO.

Two . . yes . . . [*He is disturbed by another roar of merriment from the salon.*]

MARTA.

Aren't you drinking?

MICUCCIO.

Yes . . . Right away . . .

MARTA.

Don't mind them . . . They're laughing, naturally . . . There's so many of them there . . . My dear boy, that's life. What can a person do? Her career . . . It's the impresario . . .

DORINA.

[*Reappears with another course.*]

MARTA.

Here, Dorina . . . Let me have your plate, Micuccio . . . You'll like this . . . [*Serving.*] Tell me how much you want . . .

MICUCCIO.

As you please. . .

MARTA.

[*As above.*]

Here you are. [*Serves herself. Dorina leaves.*]

MICUCCIO.

How well you've learned! You make my eyes bulge with astonishment!

MARTA.

I had to, my boy.

MICUCCIO.

When I saw you come in with that velvet cloak on your back . . . and that hat on your head . . .

MARTA.

Necessity, my son!

MICUCCIO.

I understand . . . eh! You must keep up appearances! But if they ever saw you dressed like that in Palma, *zia* Marta . . .

MARTA.

[*Hiding her face in her hands.*]

Oh, good heavens, don't mention it! Believe
me . . . whenever I think of it . . . shame . . .
shame overwhelms me! . . . I look at myself. I
say, "Is this really I, so bedizened?" . . . And it
seems that it's all a make-believe . . . as in the
carnival season . . . But what's a person to do?
Necessity, my son!

MICUCCIO.

Of course . . . certainly . . . once you get into
that life . . . But, she's really 'way up in the world,
hey? . . . You can see that — really 'way up? . . .
They . . . they pay her well, eh?

MARTA.

Oh, yes . . . Very well. . .

MICUCCIO.

How much per performance?

MARTA.

It depends. According to the seasons and the
theatres, you see. . . But let me tell you, my boy,
it costs money. Ah, how much it costs, this life we
lead. . . It takes all the money we can get! If you
only knew the enormous expenses! It all goes out
as fast as it comes in. . . Clothes, jewels, expenses
of every sort. . . [*A loud outburst of voices in the
salon at the rear cuts her short.*]

Voices.

Where? Where? Where? We want to know! Where?

Sina's Voice.

A moment! I tell you, only a moment!

Marta.

There! That's she! . . . Here she comes. . .

Sina.

[*She comes hastening in, rustling with silk, sparkling with gems, her shoulders, bosom and arms bare. It seems as if the hallway has suddenly been flooded with light.*]

Micuccio.

[*Who had just stretched his hand out toward the wine glass, sits transfixed, his face flaming, his eyes distended, his mouth agape, dazzled and stupefied, as if in the presence of a vision. He stammers.*]

Teresina. . .

Sina.

Micuccio? Where are you? Ah, there he is. . . Oh, how are things? Are you all better now? Fine, fine. . . You were so sick, weren't you? Oh, I'll see you again soon. . . Mamma will stay with you in the meantime. . . Agreed, eh? See you later. [*Dashes out.*]

Micuccio.

[*Stands amazed, while the reappearance of Sina in the salon is greeted with loud shouts.*]

MARTA.

[*After a long silence, in order to break the stupefaction into which he has fallen.*]

Aren't you eating?

MICUCCIO.

[*Looks at her stupidly, without understanding.*]

MARTA.

Eat. [*pointing to the plate.*]

MICUCCIO.

[*Inserts two fingers between his neck and his
begrimed, wilted collar, tugging at it as if to
make room for a deep breath.*]

Eat? [*His fingers drum against his chin as if in
self-confessed refusal, to signify: "I've lost my appetite, I can't." For a while he is silent, overwhelmed,
absorbed in the vision that has just left him, then he
murmurs:*] What she's come to! . . . It . . . it
doesn't seem true. . . All . . . in that style. . .
[*He refers, without scorn, but rather in a stupor, to
Sina's nudity.*] A dream. . . Her voice. . . Her
eyes. . . It's no longer she. . . Teresina. . . [*Real-
izing that ZIA Marta is shaking her head sadly, and
that she, too, has stopped eating, as if waiting for him.*]
Fie! . . . No use thinking about it. . . It's all
over. . . Who knows how long since! . . . And I,
fool that I was . . . stupid. . . They had told me
so back in the country . . . and I . . . broke my
bones to get here. . . Thirty-six hours on the
train . . . all for the sake of making a laughing-

stock of myself . . . for that waiter and that maid there . . . Dorina. . . How they laughed! . . . I, and . . . [*Several times he brings his forefingers together, as a symbol of his union with Sina, and smiles in melancholy fashion, shaking his head.*] But what else was I to believe? I came because you . . . Teresina, had . . . had promised me. . . But perhaps . . . Yes, that's it . . . How was she herself to imagine that one fine day she'd be where she is now? While I . . . yonder . . . stayed behind . . . with my piccolo . . . in the town square. . . She . . . making such strides. . . Lord! . . . No use thinking of that. . . [*He turns, somewhat brusquely, and faces ZIA Marta.*] If I have done anything for her, nobody *zia* Marta, must suspect that I have come to . . . to stay. . . [*He grows more and more excited, and jumps to his feet.*] Wait! [*He thrusts a hand into his coat pocket and pulls out a pocketbook.*] I came just for this: to give you back the money you sent to me. Do you want to call it a payment? Restitution? What's the difference! I see that Teresina has become a . . . a queen! I see that . . . nothing! Let's drop it! But this money, no! I didn't deserve that from you . . . What's the use! It's all over, so let's forget it . . . But money? No! Money to me? Nothing doing! I'm only sorry that the amount isn't complete . . .

MARTA.

[*Trembling, shattered, tears in her eyes.*]

What are you saying, my boy? What are you saying?

MICUCCIO.

[*Signals her to be quiet.*]

It wasn't I who spent it. My parents spent it while I was sick, without my knowledge. But let that make up for the tiny amount I spent for her in the early days . . . Do you remember? It's a small matter . . . Let's forget it. Here's the rest. And I'm going.

MARTA.

What do you mean! So suddenly? Wait at least until I can tell Teresina. Didn't you hear her say that she wanted to come back? I'll go right away and tell her . . .

MICUCCIO.

[*Holding her back in her seat.*]

No. It's useless. Understand?

[*From the salon comes the sound of a piano and of voices singing a silly, salacious chorus from a musical comedy, punctuated by outbursts of laughter.*]

Let her stay there . . . She's in her element, where she belongs . . . Poor me . . . I've seen her. That was enough . . . Or rather . . . you better go there . . . Do you hear them laughing? I don't want them to laugh at me . . . I'm going . . .

MARTA.

[*Interpreting Micuccio's sudden resolution in the worse sense, that is, as an attitude of scorn and an access of jealousy.*]

But I . . . It's impossible for me to keep watch over her any more, my dear boy . . .

MICUCCIO.

[*All at once reading in her eyes the suspicion that he has not yet formed, his face darkens and he cries out.*]

Why?

MARTA.

[*Bewildered, she hides her face in her hands but cannot restrain the rush of tears, as she gasps between sobs.*]

Yes, yes. Go, my boy, go . . . She's no longer fit for you. You're right . . . If you had only taken my advice . . .

MICUCCIO.

[*With an outburst, bending over her and tearing one of her hands from her face.*]

Then . . . Ah, then she . . . she is no longer worthy of me! [*The chorus and the tones of the piano continue.*]

MARTA.

[*Weeping and in anguish, she nods yes, then raises her hands in prayer, in so supplicating, heartbroken a manner that Micuccio's rage at once subsides.*]

For mercy's sake, for mercy's sake! For pity of me, Micuccio mine!

Micuccio.

Enough, enough . . . I'm going just the same . . . I'm all the more determined, now . . . What a fool I was, *zia* Marta, not to have understood. All for this . . . all . . . all naked . . . Don't cry . . . What's to be done about it? It's luck . . . luck . . . [*As he speaks, he takes up his valise and the little bag and starts to leave. It suddenly occurs to him that inside of the little bag there are the beautiful limes that he had brought from Sicily for Teresina.*] Oh, look, *zia* Marta. . . Look here . . . [*Opens the bag and supporting it on his arm pours out upon the table the fresh, fragrant fruit.*]

Marta.

Limes! Our beautiful limes!

Micuccio.

I had brought them for her . . . [*He takes one.*] Suppose I were to start throwing them at the heads of all those fine gentlemen in there?

Marta.

[*Again beseeching him.*]

For mercy's sake!

Micuccio.

[*With a bitter laugh, thrusting the empty bag into his pocket.*]

No, nothing. Don't be afraid. I leave them for you alone, *zia* Marta. And tell them I paid the duty on them, too . . . Enough. They're for you only, remember that. As to her, simply say, for me, "The best of luck to you!"

> [*He leaves. The chorus continues. ZIA Marta is left weeping alone before the table, her face buried in her hands. A long pause, until Sina Marnis takes it into her head to make another fleeting appearance in the hallway.*]

Sina.

> [*Surprised, catching sight of her weeping mother.*]

Has he gone?

Marta.

> [*Without looking at her, nods yes.*]

Sina.

> [*Stares vacantly ahead of her, engrossed, then with a sigh.*]

The poor fellow . . .

Marta.

Look . . . He had brought you . . . some limes.

Sina.

> [*Her spirits returning.*]

Oh, how beautiful! Just see . . . how many! What fragrance! How beautiful, beautiful! [*She presses one arm to her waist and in her other hand seizes as many as she can carry, shouting to the guests in the salon, who come running in.*] Didì! Didì! Rosì! Gegè! Cornelli! Tarini! Didì!

MARTA.

[*Rising in vehement protest.*]

No! Not there! I say no! Not there!

SINA.

[*Shrugging her shoulders and offering the fruit to the guests.*]

Let me do as I please! Here, Didì! Sicilian limes! Here's some for you, Rosì, Sicilian limes! Sicilian limes!*

CURTAIN.

*The new version (1920) has a different ending. Sina, instead of gaily distributing the limes to her guests, stands in tears before her former sweetheart, who repudiating her remorse, thrusts the money into her bosom and leaves.